THE ART THEATER

The Guild Theater, home of the New York Theater Guild. At once the most complete art theater "plant" in the United States and one of the best tangible evidences of the progress made by the institutional theaters in the last decade. (Crane, Franzheim and Bettis, Architects.)

THE ART THEATER

ITS CHARACTER AS DIFFERENTIATED FROM THE COMMERCIAL THEATER; ITS IDEALS AND ORGANIZATION; AND A RECORD OF CERTAIN EUROPEAN AND AMERICAN EXAMPLES

BY SHELDON CHENEY

REVISED AND ENLARGED EDITION
With sixteen new illustrations

NEW YORK ALFRED · A · KNOPF MCMXXV

SET UP, ELECTROTYPED AND PRINTED BY THE VAIL-BALLOU PRESS, INC., BINGHAMTON, N. Y. · ESPARTO PAPER MANUFACTURED IN SCOTLAND AND FURNISHED BY W. F. ETHERINGTON & COMPANY, NEW YORK · BOUND BY H. WOLFF ESTATE, NEW YORK.

MANUFACTURED IN THE UNITED STATES OF AMERICA

CONTENTS

PREFACE 1

I. PRESENT CONDITIONS IN THE AMERICAN THEATER 15

Meaning and place of the Art Theater—As differentiated from the commercial theater—The speculative theater and profits—Insurgent playhouses of two sorts: our merely little theaters and our youthful art theaters—How the American theater became commercialized—Effects upon playwriting, acting and stagecraft—Need for a new theater—Outline of the insurgent movement

II. THE COMING OF THE ART THEATER: EUROPE 37

The American problem in the light of Europe's theaters of forty years ago—The *Théâtre Libre* movement—Its service in ridding the theater of artificiality and deadening traditions—Its shortcomings—Beginnings of the art theater movement—Gordon Craig—Adolphe Appia—The Moscow Art Theater—The Munich Art Theater—Max Reinhardt and the *Deutsches Theater*—The Abbey Theater—Jacques Copeau—Effects of the movement on the European theatrical situation

III. THE COMING OF THE ART THEATER: AMERICA 62

The New Theater failure—America's first steps toward the art theater type, in New York, Chicago and Detroit—The Theater Guild—The Actors' Theater—The Provincetown Players—The Neighborhood Playhouse and the Western Community Theaters

IV. IDEALS OF THE ART THEATER 83

Idealism as an ideal—The distinguishing mark of art theater production—The synthetic ideal—Appia's inner unity—Craig's synthesis of movement, light, color and sound—Stylization—The ideal of experimentation—The ideal of sound management—The ideal of intimacy—The repertory ideal—Pursuing art theater ideals

V. THE ARTIST-DIRECTOR 106

Enlightened artist-directors our first need—Craig's ideal artist of the theater—Huntly Carter's ideal of group direction—The practical figure—Max Reinhardt—The German *regisseur*—Jessner and others—American examples—On Broadway—The little theater directors

VI. THE QUESTION OF ACTING AND ACTORS 133

Not a theoretical treatise—State of American acting—Beauty of speech—Rhythm of movement—Group action and pictorial composition—Ensemble acting—The curse of personality—Where do our actors come from?—The little theaters and amateur acting—Professionalizing amateurs—The amateurs of Moscow and Dublin—The actor under the art theater—Betterment of the actor's economic status under the Actors' Equity Association—Repertory advantages

VII. THE QUESTION OF PLAYS 161

The art theater play and the journalistic drama—The "advanced" ideal and "pleasing the public"—Sam Hume's theory—Analysis of plays at representative little and art theaters—Maurice Browne and the no-compromise attitude—Catholic choice of plays—The classics homeless in America—Poetic and realistic plays—Plays growing out of the art theaters—Native and foreign plays—Encouraging the native writer—The repertory system—The author and standards of production

VIII. THE QUESTION OF STAGE SETTINGS 186

Stage decoration and the art theater ideal—In the bad old days—Belasco and the naturalistic revolt—The artists' revolt—The improved painted setting—The plastic setting—The decorative setting—Stylization—Conventions—Light and color—Craig's screens—Hume's adaptable setting for little theaters

IX. THE QUESTION OF AUDIENCES AND THE COMMUNITY 208

Relation between theater and community—Organizing audiences without supplying theaters—Difference between New York and provinces—Defining a community theater—

Pasadena and Santa Barbara Community Theaters—Advantages of the subscription system—The Theater Guild audience—The Berlin Volksbühne—Extension work through schools and colleges—Theaters as social centers—The Neighborhood Playhouse and its community—Relation between Provincetown Players and Broadway

X. ORGANIZATION AND MANAGEMENT 228

Lack of business efficiency in little theaters—Sound management—The three-fold system of organization—The controlling group—Questions of ownership—The artist-director—The business manager—System in handling money and book-keeping—Budget-making—Income and expenditures during sample seasons on and off Broadway—Managing the art theater—Advertising and critics—Endowment—Freedom from interference under subsidy

XI. BUILDINGS AND EQUIPMENT 253

The art theater and theater architecture—The architecture of the show business—The ideal building—Design and decoration—Stage equipment—The Guild Theater and others—Size—Dream theaters

XII. UNREALIZED IDEALS 263

On the threshold—The ideal American art theater—The way of its coming—Foundations

A DISCURSIVE BIBLIOGRAPHY 267

INDEX

ILLUSTRATIONS

The Guild Theater, New York *Frontispiece*

Scenes from *Beyond* at the Provincetown Playhouse *Opposite page* 18

Scene from *The Blue Bird* at the Moscow Art Theater 46

The Neighborhood Playhouse, New York 66

The Pasadena Community Playhouse 80

Scenes from *Malvaloca* at the Actors' Theater 94

Scenes from *Hamlet* at the *Deutsches Theater*, Berlin 112

Scene from *Grotesques* at the Chicago Little Theater 122

Scenes by Emil Pirchan for the State Theater, Munich, and the State Theater, Berlin 144

Scenes from *The Failures* as produced by the Theater Guild 164

The formal stage at the *Théâtre du Vieux Colombier* 178

Scene from *Liliom* as produced by the Theater Guild 194

Diagram of five arrangements of the permanent setting at the Arts and Crafts Theater 204

Arrangements of the permanent setting at the Arts and Crafts Theater, Detroit 206

The Volksbühne, Berlin 220

The Santa Barbara Community Theater 234

The Theater of the Golden Bough, Carmel-by-the-Sea 256

ILLUSTRATIONS

The Guild Theatre, New York . . . . *Frontispiece*
Scene from *Beyond* at the Provincetown Playhouse
Scene from *The Game* [illegible] at the [illegible] Theatre . . . 8
The Neighborhood Playhouse, New York 60
The Pasadena Community Playhouse 82
Scene from [illegible] at the Actors' Theatre . . . 94
Scene from [illegible] at the [illegible] . . . 116
Scene from [illegible]
and [illegible] 144
Scene from *The* [illegible] as produced by the Theatre
Guild 164
The [illegible] scene from *The* [illegible] . . . 176
Scene from [illegible] as produced by the [illegible] Guild . . . 194
Diagram of [illegible] of the [illegible] setting
at the [illegible] Theatre 204
Arrangement of the permanent setting [illegible]
[illegible] 209
The [illegible] 210
The Santa Barbara Community Theatre 214
The Theatre of the Golden Bough, Carmel-by-the-Sea . . 2[illegible]

PREFACE TO THE REVISED EDITION

As I sit down to the rewriting of this book, on a day in mid-April, 1925, Spring is breaking about me. I am pleased to read into the circumstance an omen and a metaphor. The world of the American art theater is at the Spring. One may discern little green shoots in bewildering number, and there is the rosy promise of blossom-buds swelling, and the smell of fertile earth newly turned.

In this metaphorical theatrical garden, to be sure, not a few of the sprouted projects are very tender and tentative, and some will succumb to the first frost. One that only recently sprang up, insufficiently rooted and under the imposing title Art Theater of New York, has but this week withered and died untimely. But signs of life, birth, growth, desire, new beauty, are everywhere. Even in the rigorous climate of New York one may detect several surprising examples of hardihood and persistence and recurrent flowing of sap. And under the more kindly circumstances of life in California, I am led to believe, the seasonal little theaters not only have taken deeper root than ever before, but Burbanklike, have come to flourish unashamedly as evergreens of the first order.

It was almost exactly ten years ago, in that same California, that I began the writing of this book about the creative as distinguished from the business theater. I had been interested in a project for a producing theater in Berkeley (a sprout that was badly frost-bitten shortly thereafter, despite the climate), and I knew something about the Greek Theater productions at the University of California, and the experiments at the San Francisco and Los Angeles Little Theaters. The following year I became implicated in the first season of productions at the Arts and Crafts Theater in Detroit, and also found time for first-hand observation of the work of the Chicago Little Theater, the Washington Square Players and the Neighborhood Playhouse. Concurrently I was reading avidly anything that I could find in print about the art theaters of Europe. The completion and publication of *The Art Theater* followed shortly afterward, in 1917, partly as a summary of my observation and study, partly as a permanent record of the Arts and Crafts venture.

Taking up in 1925 the task of rewriting the book to chronicle later progress, I look back at the intervening eight or ten years with a feeling akin to amazement. The independent theaters, the progressive and creative stages, the insurgent producing groups, as viewed collectively from a window not far distant from Broadway, may still seem in general very new, very tentative, far from artistic maturity; but since 1915 they have multiplied wondrously, and a few examples of the true institutional theater have emerged, to be a permanent reminder of progress, to prove the lasting productiveness of the new spirit, to serve their communities continuously and well. These firmly established progressive theaters, moreover, are now not only accepted but considered respectable in their several communities, and already they have made theatrical history.

The groups that can conceivably be bedded together —in the garden, of course—under the title "art theaters," have made history in two directions. On Broadway, in the very center of the commercial amusement market place, they have not been content to remain merely a *threat* to the old order—which was the best we could claim for them a decade ago—but have become competitors in a particularly disagreeable and menacing way: with menace of better grade goods offered with greater assurance of permanent satisfaction to the consumer. They have incidentally taken over a considerable number of regular playhouses, and are building others.

In the other direction, away from Broadway, they have retrieved innumerable barns, barrooms, churches, studios, and other odds and ends of civilized building, all the way from Maine to California, from crowded sophisticated Greenwich Village to the open spaces of Vancouver, and in these they have rigged up every conceivable sort of possible and impossible stage, and are giving hundreds of plays thereon every week, plays from the Greek and the Japanese and the Czecho-Slovakian and the Hindu and the English—even American plays. This double-directioned group movement, embracing perhaps five hundred producing outfits, is collectively our insurgent theater, and in its best manifestations our art theater.

It is not only in its production work that the insurgent theater has caught the imagination of the country. Witness the reflection of its activities at the universities, schools and public libraries, and in the publishers' lists. Colleges are endowed in its name, there are a score of summer sessions devoted to spreading its gospel, its own particular magazine has become a monthly with a world circulation, and American book publishers put forth book after book dependent upon the creative dramatic reader: volumes on the changing drama and on European stagecraft, on Stanislavsky and on Reinhardt and on a project of Geddes', on the Russian stage and the Charleston stage and Gordon Craig's stage. These all are signs of life, development, building. They indicate, if you will let me make the inference, that young America has turned to the theater for deeper experience of living and for experience of beauty. To that extent the new theater movement has become an extraordinary and vital part in the country's cultural life.

Of the *little* theaters of ten years ago I wrote in my original preface:

"In spite of the indefiniteness of aim in such theaters, and the patent instability of their organization, I became convinced that in their activities lay the only real promise of a better dramatic art in this country. Because their roots were in native soil, I felt that here were beginnings of true community theaters—which collectively would be our ultimate national theater. And because they were in the hands of artists, who, if immature and unsteady, were still sincere and forward-looking, these playhouses seemed clearly the forerunners of an American art theater."

I can freely endorse that statement to-day, as regards the majority of little theaters. They seem to me still immature, unsteady, and indefinite in aim; and individually most of them are unimportant and negligible. But collectively they are important beyond measure, building the foundations of maturer creative theaters, developing audiences for the ultimate national theater, and graduating their more ambitious workers into the groups that are seriously concerned with the search for an art theater technique and with permanent establishment of institutional theaters. They should be tended with every consideration, encouraged, nourished, not only because they thus are incubators for the next generation of professional theater artists, but because to-day they are the only means by which drama is brought to hundreds of towns and hundreds of thousands of people. No picture of such organizations as the Theater Guild and the Cleveland Playhouse and the Pasadena Community Theater, moreover, is complete without its background embracing the panorama of these ambitious ventures.

Because the real fight for an art theater in America, a theater dominating the dramatic entertainment situation, seems to me now to lie in a field where professional standards are rightly demanded, and professional workers employed, I shall have the less to say about the provincial background groups, being principally concerned with the dozen organizations that have come closest to the permanency of institutions. But that living background is always in my mind, and should be in the reader's.

It is naturally in New York that the new spirit has brought its manifestations into competition with the professional-commercial producers. And I am turning there for the most vivid illustration of the concrete change accomplished in the decade. Ten years ago three or four insurgent groups were experimenting more or less seriously in New York despite the scorn of the "regular" managers and the neglect or the barbed wit of the reviewers. David Belasco (the same who now is the patron saint of the annual Little Theater Tournaments) had gone out of his way to write: "Some one should arise and speak the truth . . . Theaters and acting organizations devoted to false ideals are not new, but never, until this season, have they been so vicious, vulgar and degrading. They have multiplied alarmingly . . . This so-called new art of the theater is but a flash in the pan of inexperience. It is the cubism of the theater—the wail of the incompetent and degenerate . . . The whole thing merely shows an ignorance and a diseased and depraved understanding and appreciation of any art at all." No one—not even those of us who were writing enthusiastically of the promise of the new movement—dared prophesy that non-commercial organizations would in a decade be offering their productions side by side with the producing managers, and slowly but unquestionably taking over the best audiences.

This week (mid-April) if I am so minded I can see thirteen plays in New York offered by typical "organizational" theaters. The five organizations which have produced these plays are built on the foundations laid by the unstable and "incompetent" little and experimental playhouses of ten years ago. Of the thirteen plays, nine are housed in regular Broadway theaters, another is in a well-appointed playhouse in Greenwich Village, and the eleventh is at an ideal small playhouse on the East Side. Eleven of the plays are offered at regular evening engagements, with the usual eight performances a week; the other two are special matinee bills. The thirteen plays include two by Bernard Shaw, one by Ibsen, one by Congreve, one by Eugene O'Neill, one by Charles Rann Kennedy, one by Franz Molnar, a famous pantomime, a bill of dance dramas, a new English play, and native plays by three of the most promising new American playwrights, John Howard Lawson, Hatcher Hughes and Sidney Howard. The producers of these plays are the Theater Guild, the Actors' Theater, the Provincetown Players, the Neighborhood Playhouse and the Stagers.

Any mature-minded New York theatergoer will agree that he has found the majority of his memorable experiences of the current season at the performances of plays given by these non-commercial groups. For sheer theatric merit one would have to search diligently among all the other offerings on Broadway to match the small list comprised in the Guild's current four attractions, *The Wild Duck* and *Candida* as revived by the Actors' Theater, and the Provincetown Players' production of *Desire under the Elms.* Four of these plays, by the way, have already run engagements of from three to six months—indication enough that the threat of the new theater is no less marked in its economic than in its artistic aspect.

At the same time there are only three or four productions offered by the old-time managers which might conceivably challenge comparison with the average best offered by the organizations. The two that might be named unhesitatingly are productions of those two managers whom we all looked to as leaders among the regulars ten years ago: Arthur Hopkins with *What Price Glory?* and Winthrop Ames with a play by Galsworthy. The record as a whole, however, is a clear indication that *domination* in the field of the finer things in theatrical production in New York has passed from the regulars to the insurgents. If there is need for more evidence, it can be found in the fact that the Guild and the Actors' Theater have Broadway homes the year 'round, and the Provincetown Players hold two houses downtown and the Neighborhood one; whereas almost the only producing manager who still considers it worth while to have a "home theater," where a set standard constantly prevails, is David Belasco. And his houses, the Belasco and the Lyceum, have been dedicated nearly all season to two of the most inexcusably salacious plays of recent times, a vulgarized version of a comedy by Vajda, and a shocker called *Ladies of the Evening*, wherein the ways of the common prostitute are particularized upon as never before on the stage. I do not wish to suggest that this bit of pandering is typical of the surviving commercial managers; but in connection with Belasco's vaunted leadership of the American stage, and his position as almost the sole survivor of the theater-owner-producer, it is a vivid illustration of the change we are studying. One may be forgiven for recalling just at this juncture what Mr. Belasco said nine years ago about the productions of the organizational theaters being vicious, vulgar and degrading.

To what purpose have I thus recounted the play program in New York during this particular current week? Because if one grasps its significance, one is enabled to measure concretely the extent of the change that has come with the passing of a decade of struggle by the insurgents. One sees that what ten years ago was the province of Winthrop Ames, Arthur Hopkins, and less certainly of the Frohmans and Fiske and Belasco, has become more correctly the province of "outsiders"—of men working coöperatively, who do not play the game in the accepted way, either for financial profit or for personal aggrandizement, but primarily for the sake of theater art and the audience. In the same time, take note, the American stage has gained immeasurably in vitality, in talent, in world importance and prestige.

The organization theaters are not likely to have eleven or ten or six plays on Broadway continuously this season, or next season or the next; but they have shown that their time is inevitably coming.

And yet—let us not be too enthusiastic or too content with the progress that has been made lately on Broadway. We have not in America a single important professional acting company, permanently organized and permanently housed, under the leadership of a recognized artist-director. We have not a *repertory* company worthy of the name. If we did not know that the change for the better had been extraordinary in ten years, or twenty, in the matters of shift of leadership and birth of a new spirit and independence of thought, we might all very well be humble and ashamed at the lack of one permanent art theater acting company in these United States.

It is, then, the story of the rise of a new spirit, new leadership and courageous experiment, rather than the consummation of an ideal, that I am setting out to chronicle, somewhat sketchily and briefly, in the following pages, together with excursion pictures of those permanent art theater companies of Europe which are likely to prove most suggestive in our pioneer and experimental days.

. . . .

I might call the thing I am talking about by some other name than "art theater" if that phrase did not happen to describe with more exactness than any other what I am talking about. I am fully conscious of the risks one takes with those to whom the word "art" implies poseurs, academicians and "highbrows." I know particularly that a group of our superior, sophisticated

New York critics have affected a journalistic lowbrowism and have made a pose of being bored by anything that carries the art label or the special quality of detached spirituality or the mood of contemplation. I think, however, that we of the theater have arrived at a position where we should be able to use the word without self-consciousness. Then, too, the Moscow Art Theater company has been here to give to critics and theater workers some sort of concrete definition.

The term as applied to a theater group or a theater institution merely indicates that that group or institution is striving to serve its audiences with theatrical productions that are the most expressive, the truest to the theater and life of the time, that living artists—actors, scene-designers, directors—can evolve. The term "art theater" need not imply any narrow preoccupation with one code, one method, one theory—as naturalism, symbolism, the presentational drama, or stylization. The art theater is the home of the living theatrical arts, the home of stage creativeness.

. . . .

If I have given the impression in any of the paragraphs above that the prophecies I was rash enough to make in my first edition, about the development of the little theaters and art theaters of America, have come true, let me hasten to make damaging admissions. Primarily I was wrong in that I did not foresee such quick and decisive gains in the field of the professional theater; I thought the outsiders would (and perhaps should) take longer to invade Broadway and dominate the "better production" field there. I was less happily mistaken about some minor matters of acting, playwrights and plays. When, indeed, I now read over some parts of the original book, I am likely to mutter: "God save us from our past performances." I actually squirm under some instances of my own intolerance; and certainly there will be far fewer places in the following pages where I shall lay down the law didactically about what the art theater *must* do. There will also be less talk about mood and suggestion—we are ready for something more direct, stronger, harder. . . .

Well, the book served its purpose in some directions, contributed its bit to progress, as I happen happily to know; and it was all *substantially* true. Perhaps an author who writes on timely and changing subjects, who is himself changing or shifting, ought to license his books for only ten years' existence, to be recalled then for burning on appearance of a new—and of course much better—edition.

What has been added in this enlarged edition, besides fifteen new illustrations, is, of course, chiefly the story of the Theater Guild, the Actors' Theater, and the later years of the Provincetown Players and the Neighborhood Playhouse. In imbedding this material into my essay, I am also trying to push back into proper perspective the story of the Chicago Little Theater and the Detroit Arts and Crafts Theater. New references to the little theaters in the neighborhood of New York are largely based on personal observance. But I have kept my contact with the often-mentioned community theaters in California and the producing groups in the Middle West only at second hand, by meetings with the directors and reports in *Theater Arts Magazine.* I have been to Europe to check up my accounts of some of the European art theaters. And finally—last self-recommendation!—I have served for the last two and a half years in various departments, and latterly as one of the executives, of the Actors' Theater in New York. If I seem to some prejudiced, this will doubtless explain the reason; though I hope it may give to others confidence that I am no longer the fool theorist, blind with ignorance of things as they are, that some cheerfully candid critic once called me.

CHAPTER I

PRESENT CONDITIONS IN THE AMERICAN THEATER

What is the meaning of the term "Art Theater"?

What is the art theater's place?

Why should any attempt be made to differentiate the art theater from the total collective theater as it exists, say, in London or on New York's Broadway or at the Opera House in Kokomo?

In briefest statement an art theater might be defined as a theater dedicated to creative staging of important plays. Many other definitions would serve as well. From the audience's viewpoint, an art theater implies a playhouse permanently established, where a spectator can go always with the assurance of seeing fine plays of the past or present beautifully acted and adequately staged. From the viewpoint of the artist-producer, the art theater is a place where the arts of the theater are creatively practiced, free alike from the will of the businessman, from the demands of movie-minded audiences, and from the fetters of superstitious traditionalism; he probably entertains, moreover, a vision of the several contributive arts of the playwright, the actor and the designer brought together in a union or synthesis, and in the final result invariably stamped with the style or the brilliance or the quality of his own mind or imagination—this viewpoint implying an æsthetic policy and a lasting association of creative workers under artist-leadership. Theatrically moving plays, plays that widen the horizon of life, plays that stir the emotions and enrich the adult mind; ensemble acting, inspired acting, a standard of speech; reinforcement of the playwright's and the actor's effectiveness by adequate and at times beautiful setting, costuming and lighting; all these are implications of the "art" theater name. There is also this: the art theater, if it is to be distinguished from the *museum* theater, the theater run by national academicians—the Comédie Française, for example—is a living thing, pulsing with the blood of the times, true to the life and the stage of the present (not of a quarter-century ago), and expressive in the forms of that life and stage. In this view it also has a duty as the home of theatrical experiment, of the search for new beauty, as the home of progressive thought among playwrights, directors, actors and designers.

The *place* of the art theater is, speaking physically, in every community that has grown up culturally, wherever there are enough adult-minded people to form a reasonable audience. Not every town that supports a moving-picture palace is ripe for an institutional theater in the legitimate field. A great many people can understand the pictures—especially the sort they get—who cannot be considered to have the mature mentality or natural receptiveness which brings enjoyment of many of the plays typical of repertory theaters. I think, however, that any city that has in the past supported a first-class theater playing one-week engagements of touring companies, would, after a proper period of try-out and introduction, be able to support an economically administered art theater.

The place of such a theater in the dramatic scheme of a larger city—from New York to San Francisco, say—will be somewhat that of an oasis. Nothing can stem the tide of commercial production (nor should it be stemmed); and nothing short of a revolution in educational methods in our schools can make the average big-city audience less cheap-minded, less sensation-craving. So long as education tends to destroy instead of conserve imagination, emotional receptiveness and expressiveness, and independence of thought, the disease of art-blindness will remain prevalent among the great majority of good citizens. But in every large city there are enough people to make up the requisite subscription audience for the other sort of theater, if once they come to know that a standard of excellence has really been established at a certain playhouse. I believe that there is room in New York for a dozen theaters playing such programs as those offered by the Theater Guild and the Actors' Theater this season—a dozen oases among the three-score Broadway houses. If run for the best interests of their audiences and their own future development, these theaters will never make great profits (looking for "best-seller" plays is still one of the besetting sins of even the most advanced groups in New York). They will leave the obviously commercial play to their frankly and exclusively commercial competitors, and they will emphasize that theirs is a more or less idealistic, specialized, and creative sort of quest.

Why differentiate the art theater from the general run of theaters? Why not merely bring an art standard to producing as it is practiced by the Shuberts, by Brady, by A. H. Woods? In the first place, there is the matter of permanence—and the matter of continuous production. An institutional theater has the virtue of being so grounded in community life that it goes on despite the passing of one man or a dozen. It has a program which brings a certain number of performances to its audiences each year. The speculative manager drops any play, no matter how fine, if it does not show an immediate profit, and drops it permanently. And he may go through a whole season without offering a play "because conditions aren't right." One may fairly ask, right for whom?

There are dangers, of course, in over-institutionalizing. But the danger to the art values of a play at the Moscow Art Theater, the Volksbühne or even the Theater Guild is hardly so terrifying as the danger to those values in the hectic play-mill that is Broadway.

As a matter of fact the characteristics of the typical art theater are so radically different from the type theater of America that the differentiation is already made except for those who do not wish to recognize it. The aims of the "radicals" are so alien to the existing order, their willingness to sacrifice real profits to notions of art is so far beyond understanding, that it

Two scenes from *Beyond* as produced at the Provincetown Playhouse, New York. The settings, by Robert Edmond Jones, illustrate the trend toward scenic simplification and stylization in which the experimental art theater groups have pioneered. (Photographs by Francis Bruguiere.)

should be clear that never the twain shall meet. "What I see on the box office statement, I can understand," says a fellow-worker who has taught me much about Broadway. Then, too, there is the example of the several European playhouses that have proclaimed themselves "Art Theaters" in their very titles, and proved by their contributions beyond argument that there is something new in the dramatic world, beyond anything that Mr. Shubert, Mr. Brady, Mr. Woods and Mr. Belasco have ever accomplished. The Moscow Art Theater particularly, by reason of its conquests at home and then in country after country outside Russian borders, has set a standard in both production and organization that has inspired progressive workers everywhere with visions of a new and different theater.

Ten years ago, with the Moscow Art Theater in mind as a type, I was able to say that the art theater had no past in America. To-day that statement would not strictly hold. We have had beginnings to record, as I noted in my preface; and we have several "home" theaters where the effort is being made to establish the type permanently. If I speak half-heartedly, it is because I so keenly feel that true and continuous art-theater results are primarily the product of continued association together of a group of actors and artists in a permanent *company*, and that this company must be kept constantly up to its best level of performance through a repertory system of presentation.

I

The insiders, the regulars, the workers in and the manipulators of the business theater, will always consider the workers in the insurgent theaters "outsiders"—no matter how many Broadway houses the Actors' Theater, the Guild and the Provincetown Players may take over or build. They may be puzzlingly on the inside, as regards their presence, the audiences that flock to their auditoriums, and Mr. Shubert's willingness to book their "successful" shows over the regular circuits; but they certainly are not "in the game." It is as insiders and outsiders, then, that I shall describe their respective places in the American scene as it exists.

The "inside" thing, the American commercial theater, organized throughout the country as shrewdly, as ruthlessly, as the production, distribution and sales-control of gasoline or aluminum, is conducted as a speculative business, with its first object the making of profits. It would be idle to say that it has nothing to do with art, since that is in one sense the sole commodity in which it deals; but its art is the art of commerce, the art that will please the greatest number of average people, the art that finds its appeal in sentiment and prettiness and sexual emotion and situations begetting uncontrolled laughter—a sort of *Cosmopolitan-Snappy-Stories-Ladies'-Home-Journal* art. Insofar as it touches within the boundaries of the art that is both true to life and spiritual, it is most likely to do so through chance inspiration and accidental coördination.

Occasionally one sees in a Broadway theater a production which evokes that mood which is a response to art alone. But the next fifteen or twenty productions are so completely innocent of any suspicion of spiritual values that one is forced to put down the exception as a random thrust. In the end it always comes back to the same analysis: the American commercial theater is organized to earn profits in competition, and its art will always be pulled down to that standard which experience has shown will please the largest group of money-spenders.

In the field of realistic drama its standard will be pulled down to sensational plays like *Ladies of the Evening* and *The Good Bad Woman*, where the exhibition of suggestive situations or downright obscenity is excused by the producer with a show of sentimental morality at the end; or to journalistically absorbing but shallow adventure and heart-interest plays like *Rain* and *Within the Law.*

In the field of "grand drama" and spectacle it will be pulled down to the level of *Chu Chin Chow* and similar sublimated piffle. In the field of comedy it will be pulled over into farce or into sweet and innocuous Golden comedies. The art that goes beyond the obvious will be discouraged; the art that reaches down to deeper truths or touches upon unaccustomed planes of experience will be avoided; the art that arrives by new modes of expression will go unrecognized.

The producers insist, of course, and not without some justification, that they are only giving what the public demands. There can be no doubt that there is an immense dull-minded, sensation-craving audience, no less in the group of money-spenders able to pay from $2.75 to $5.50 for a seat than in the fifty-cent and one-dollar class. The half-educated product of our stereotyped grade schools; the newly rich; the sentimental ladies; the merely restless-minded with no other resources for amusement; the perpetual seeker after the latest display of gowns, the least reticent display of flesh, the parade of notorious names, the newest nerve-shocker: these doubtless are in every big-town audience, and to all of them the producing managers trim their appeal in one way or another. The New York audience, which is unfortunately the producer's gauge of the country's taste, is further vulgarized by a constant stream of travelers on holiday, convention delegates temporarily freed from home restraint, out-of-town buyers being jovially entertained by local salesmen, rich provincials wanting something startling to talk about when they return home—all in the spirit of "seeing the sights" of the big town. New York, moreover, has in its own population probably the largest lobster-eating, jazz-driven, sophisticated bloc of artificial livers in the world, a great many of them apartmented in the Forties along Broadway. They have the money, the producer correctly opines. And he chooses his plays according.

Two criticisms can be validly made regarding this policy. First, a moderate-sized, thoroughly intelligent, decent-minded audience is always available in New York, made up of both local residents and a number of travelers who go traveling precisely to find the best. This audience may not alone be able to put a play in the "best-seller" class, but it is encouragingly large, and increasing. In the second place, if the managers try to use lockout tactics to control the *entire* theater supply, thus taking over the institution as both an art and a business, they have no right to gauge the quality of their offered goods solely by the lowest common denominator of the demand. They have no right to play their game solely with the idea of producing a best-seller. There is nothing truer than that the offering of the finest drama creates automatically further demand for that finest. Opportunity to enjoy the best, breeds appreciation and continuous demand. It is the rare exception among the managers who looks for a play script with an eye to that opportunity and that moderate-sized audience; the average eye sees through a box office window in terms of crowd appreciation—and the play is chosen for mediocre virtues that will appeal to mediocre minds.

If our sculpture were produced under such a handicap we should never have a St. Gaudens or a Lachaise, but only a race of manipulators and imitators producing those horrid sweet statuettes which our pseudo-art stores import from Italy by the thousand, for "the art trade." And if a group of businessmen controlled all the galleries as they have controlled the theaters, we should never have a Sargent or a Davies or a Marin, but only a race of Harrison Fishers and Howard Chandler Christies and similar corrupters of the art morals of the newsstand public. The theater alone has been so fettered that it has stifled creative effort, discouraged originality, and driven out the true artist-producer.

II

In order to understand better how deep-rooted is the condition on Broadway—and why the outsiders, amateurs, radicals and experimenters found the "art" theater field practically untenanted—it is worth while to strike back a generation or two into theatrical history. Forty years ago America boasted excellent repertory and stock playhouses and great actors, and the drama gave promise of developing side by side with American sculpture, painting and architecture. Daly's company particularly was of a sort that might have served as a model through the changing years, with a resultant American institutional theater to-day worthy of the name. That company was international in reputation and an integral part of the creative life of cultivated America. But before its disintegration even, the commercialization of the New York stage began.

Thirty years ago two influential managers acquired a booking agency which up to that time had been more or less of a convenience to scattered theater-owners, producers and company managers as a clearing-house to arrange routes, dates, etc. The new combination speedily absorbed rivals, and brought under its direct control a formidable string of first-class theaters. The alliance became so powerful that other managers and theater-owners joined, either in the hope of sharing the larger profits or in self-defense. The "syndicate" adopted the methods common to lawless "big business" of that day. It started a merciless compaign to stamp out competition and kill off hold-out rivals. It bribed into its ranks as many big men as it could, and then frightened into line as many more, big and little, as could be bullied. Then it fought the remaining few, managers and actors, by relentless warfare, closing theaters to them, and using all the familiar tactics of the lockout. After a short campaign so few rebels remained that the American theater lay practically helpless in the hands of a few New York speculators. No cornering of a market was ever more skillfully or completely manipulated.

Certain gains under such a monopoly are easily recognized. For owners of theaters outside New York the new system meant a continued succession of companies with tried plays, in place of the previous uncertain bookings. When rightly managed it prevented two similar and worthy productions playing in opposition one week, with an empty week following. The theater market was in a sense stabilized. And of course the combination was a success from the speculators' standpoint. Experiment was eliminated, profits formerly scattered to a hundred independent agencies now flowed regularly to the one headquarters in New York, and price-raising was possible on a cornered commodity.

It is necessary to add, before turning to the other side of the case—the losses entailed in the commercializing process—that about twenty years ago there came a revolt against the syndicate. It succeeded to the extent of opening the field to a rival business organization. The burden was partially lifted from the shoulders of the small owner of theaters on the road, and the small producer came back into the field under definite limitations. But it was distinctly a business revolt, and it failed to change conditions so far as the artist was concerned. He remained either a servant of the businessmen or an outsider. We now have had for some years two coöperating syndicates instead of one—with a breaking-up process apparently setting in very recently.

The evil effects of the system in general were: loss of freedom for the artist; destruction of the training-grounds in which both actor and playwright had formerly gained experience and early success; and ruinous control by New York over all the important theaters in the country. Repertory suffered a quick death, since one long run cost less money than frequent change of bill; and independent experiment soon disappeared. In those individual contributive arts that go to make up the larger art of the theater—playwriting, acting, staging, decoration—the havoc wrought was so great that ten years ago we had not one theater artist of any sort who was internationally important.

In the matter of playwriting, centralized control of all the theaters in the land meant standardization of types of production, so that the dramatist who brought forward anything new found every trying-out ground closed to him. "Kept" playwrights became the rule. It was easier and safer to repeat a proven formula, or adapt a foreign success, than to risk money on untried types of play. If a native playwright did get by with an undoubted success, it was easier for the manager to repeat variations on that than to give the next fellow a chance. Such a false standard of lavish, if artistically doubtful, staging developed, moreover, that it cost a manager a minimum of $5000 to try out a play in the usual Broadway way.* Under such a burden of expense even those producers who retained some desire to encourage native art hesitated to touch anything new. The American playwright for two decades thus was left without laboratory or studio. Only with the coming of the little theaters, and especially of such organizations as the Provincetown Players and the Wisconsin Players, was his testing-ground to some extent restored.

For the actor the conditions were—and are—even worse. The breaking up of the repertory and dignified stock companies destroyed the training school where so many of the older artists gained their most fruitful experience and inspiration. It made the living of the actor insecure, there being no longer any chance of association with the same company in a permanent home for even a season at a time. All but actors of

* To-day, in 1925, it costs far more than this to stage even a simple production "in the usual Broadway way." The decreased purchasing value of the dollar, increased theater rentals and a greater advertising tribute exacted by the newspapers have brought the minimum up to a point between $10,000 and $15,000.

the highest salary are to-day required to live lives of perpetual uncertainty, because their contracts are dependent solely upon the financial success of plays and companies chosen and presented without regard to their own preferences and ideals. They have no choice but to seek peripatetic employment under a system that makes permanent interest impossible, and one that denies leisure for proper study of their art.

But perhaps the most destructive practice in regard to acting was that of creating and exploiting "stars." The star system implies on its face an unbalanced art, in which the poor is too often placed beside the worthy. Of the stars themselves little need be said. Many of them are sterling actors, potentially much greater than their limitations in opportunity have allowed them to appear. They would show a finer talent and more versatility if they could cut loose from the system. But it cannot be insisted upon too strongly that star production is pernicious for the minor actor. Not only does it create a false ideal in the company, an ideal that impels the young actor to cultivate and parade every idiosyncrasy of personality and learn every trick which might lead to stardom, but it almost inevitably deadens originality and precludes breadth of training and understanding, by condemning the rising artist to year after year of type parts. The long run and the star system were largely responsible for that dearth of intelligent clean-speaking actors which existed on the American stage five and ten years ago.

The effect of the system in the matter of staging was

no less unfortunate than in the fields of playwriting and acting. The lack of artist-directors, which to-day seems the chief obstacle in the way of developing art theaters, is directly due to the standardization of methods in the regular theater. The businessman took control and delegated the designing of the settings to one helper, the designing of costumes to another, the stage direction to another. He insisted, moreover, that each one of these helpers do his work in a way that squared with accepted notions of stage art, in this case, of course, business art. Under such a system initiative in stagecraft was crushed, the ambitious young artist who went into the scenic studios soon became a machine, and play production in America lagged twenty years behind developments in Germany, Austria, Russia and other artistically alive countries.

Ten or twelve years ago, to be sure, the businessmen woke up to find that European theaters had discovered methods of staging infinitely better than the accepted ones, and that in this country certain little theaters and an opera house had imported or developed artists capable of creating some of "the new effects." The commercial managers immediately hired some of these artists to come to their rescue. The results were interesting from a purely decorative standpoint, but something was lacking. Broadway pieces were decked in the clothes of the new stagecraft—but remained vulgar. The point that both sides overlooked was this: these artists were able to do their best work only when they were given full charge of the production (if they were directors as well as designers), or when they worked with other artists and not with businessmen. At any rate, there were years when the spirit of the new staging was finding truer expression on small stages in Chicago and Detroit than in New York.

In one other particular the speculative system put America decades behind the best practice in Europe. In the matter of theater architecture we stumbled along in an uninspired way for many years after Littmann was revolutionizing the auditoriums of German theaters and creating a new relationship between audience and stage. Our architects were making their own helpful changes in the Italian-French structure that was so largely based on social and decorative rather than primarily theatrical ideals; but the boxes, the excessive ornament, the three-floor seating plan and other abominations persisted. Even a decade ago there were hardly a dozen theaters in America that had even been touched by strictly modern ideas of theater-building. For the most part they were vulgar amusement palaces, inexcusably gilded and red-plushed and varnished and stenciled. At their best they still seemed showy and ornate. They reflected perfectly the taste of the businessmen-owners. They were built, moreover, not to house a certain company, or to fit the requirements of any particular sort of staging, or for dignified or cheap audiences, but to accommodate *any* show that could be booked in at a profit, musical, Shakespeare, farce, or shocker. The average appeal again! And certainly not a home for art.

Such were the losses to the contributive arts, which resulted from the over-organization of the theater as a business. To these I may add one other misfortune: the people of this country lost all respect for the theater. They visualized it as a business, like insurance, or selling groceries. To be implicated in stage work even involved more or less risk of one's reputation and standing in the community. And understanding the theater to be a purely commercial and profit-making proposition, the real theater lovers gave up going to plays except on very special occasions. The best audience was alienated.

III

It took many years for critics to realize the full mischief that was being worked through the manipulation of the theater as a speculative medium. As long ago as 1900 clear-sighted commentators like Norman Hapgood threw searchlights on the situation, and Walter Prichard Eaton and others kept the issue alive. But it took many years more to learn that the theater could not be saved from within.

Some ten years ago it seemed to many of us that the normal corrective was likely to be something distinctive growing out of the little theaters, something entirely apart from the "regular" organization, something that would need endowment at first, perhaps; something primarily devoted to the arts of the stage and forgetful of great profits, and thus able to pursue its way without regard to competition. We knew, of course, that the little theaters lacked stability, business efficiency, self-confidence, and many another virtue desirable in a child to whom such ambitious hopes were attached. They were sometimes timid, frantically disclaiming any intention toward reform, and admitting only a desire to "please ourselves"; and sometimes boastful, calling attention to their littleness as if that in itself were a virtue, instead of simply a sign that they hadn't grown up. They were, nevertheless, the most hopeful sign in the theater world, because their roots were in native soil and because they were reaching up beyond those realms of commerce and materialism in which the business theater constantly existed. They were often rich, moreover, in those things that the other theater lacked: artistic taste, cultural background, creative energy, and imagination.

There had been a sudden burst of little theater activity in 1915 and 1916. The Chicago Little Theater had been established in 1912, to be sure, and had had forerunners there. The Toy Theater of Boston and the Wisconsin Dramatic Society were already much talked about as pioneers. But in 1915–16 the following very important projects came to life: the Neighborhood Playhouse, the Washington Square Players, the Los Angeles Little Theater, the Portmanteau Theater, the Provincetown Players, the Arts and Crafts Theater, the Wisconsin Players, the Players' Workshop, the Prairie Playhouse, the Cleveland Playhouse, the Indianapolis Little Theater. And there were scores of less important (or in some cases only less advertised) groups developing from coast to coast.

American participation in the war put an end to that burst of activity. But the five years since 1920 have again seen phenomenal growth and change in both little and big playhouses. In that time the American stage has developed in importance until New York leads the world in the amount of energy, effort, money and talent poured into her theaters. Europe's outstanding directors and players are brought to this country to exhibit their goods and to serve as example. Play scouts bring the latest scripts from Berlin, Prague, Paris, Budapest, Vienna. And the charge of a decade ago, that America had then not a single theater artist of international importance, is answered to-day by O'Neill plays in all the chief capitals of Europe, John Barrymore playing *Hamlet* in London, Norman Geddes and Richard Herndon in Paris on a producing project, German books and magazine articles on stage decoration with Jones, Geddes, and Simonson featured, and more American plays running in London than English plays in New York.

The post-war increase in little theater activity is no less amazing—there are at least five hundred actual amateur producing groups in the country. Perhaps their public is larger than that which goes to the big theater. They vary in standards of production, in importance of plays chosen, in number of productions offered and performances given. They vary in dependability and maturity and size. But there they are—and still growing. Their more ambitious graduates are playing with the Theater Guild, the Actors' Theater and the commercial managers. Or are designing settings for them. Or have gone out to organize and direct other little theater companies. But the great majority are home-town folks who will stay in the home town, and continue to work on the little stage there. And whether they have turned up good actors and promising playwrights or not, they are setting an average of attractive and often beautiful stage setting and lighting that would have seemed a miracle to us a dozen years ago.

IV

Last to be mentioned in this chapter on conditions in the American theater, after the commercial theaters and after the mass of little theaters, there is the group between, the real beginning art theaters. The New York group that I wrote about in the preface, the producers of those dozen or so plays that are puzzling the "regular" managers, will serve most often as examples. They too vary in dependability, maturity and size. The Theater Guild is "established" beyond any doubt, with a lavish new building of its own and two other Broadway theaters under lease—and a subscription audience that numbers at the moment 14,000. The Actors' Theater is younger, without its own home, still wobbling in policy, shifting in its personnel; but with a record of such a fine standard of production as no other organization has achieved. If it can give New York continuously such remarkable ensemble performances, whether of new native plays or classics, it can outlive many a mistake in choice of manuscript and grow old in the service of a community hungry for the rare treat of great acting. These two are the most professional, the most nearly "standard" art theaters.

The Provincetown group has reaped the reward of its own early belief in experiment and the native playwright, and is riding to success on the plays of Eugene O'Neill, despite puzzlingly poor acting standards during the current season and the one preceding. The Neighborhood Playhouse moves slowly but surely to another sort of success, more limited but equally significant, a complete success in its own little corner. And outside New York, the Pasadena and Santa Barbara Community groups have grown to such stature that they have built theaters of their own, of full professional size, ideally appointed, and not at all in the image of New York or Berlin or Paris, but in the spirit of the semi-modern, semi-traditional cultural revival on the Coast. Carmel also has its new theater building, and has called the veteran Maurice Browne to direct it. The Ram's Head Players in Washington have been operating this season in a private theater built for them on account of their past success. The Cleveland Playhouse flourishes and takes first place among producing groups between New York and the Coast, and is drawing plans for its promised model theater. Dallas, Texas, sends up to New York a Little Theater group with such living native material that it wins the Little Theater Tournament two years in succession. Chicago builds an as-yet-unopened art theater and puts the wise Thomas Wood Stevens in charge. Even Boston has under construction its so-called Repertory Theater, and tax-exempts it because it is foundation-owned and presumably a public service organization.

Even though we see that America has not yet developed one normal permanent art theater company, we have seen half a dozen near-ideal buildings erected for workers toward that goal; we have seen something approaching a distinctive art theater technique of production evolved by experimental groups; we have seen notable progress toward efficient coöperative organization; we have had one instance of a group developing a subscription audience of 14,000 members; we have seen standards of production, of acting, of playwriting, improve measurably.

These things the insurgents have done. For one who believes that the real art of the theater in America depends for its fullest development upon the emergence of fixed local playhouses with resident companies, dedicated to repertory production of both native and foreign plays, directed by artists and art-lovers rather than businessmen, the dawn has come. We are entering upon the period of full daylight. Or to return to the original metaphor, Spring is here. Summer is close behind.

CHAPTER II

THE COMING OF THE ART THEATER: EUROPE

To have an art theater in an American city, it is neither necessary nor wise to copy outright European models. The *form* of our institutional theaters must grow out of American conditions. But it is safe to say that not one of the pioneers of the progressive theater movement in this country has failed to know and to find inspiration in the outstanding art theaters of Europe. Maurice Browne, Robert Edmond Jones, Sam Hume, Augustin Duncan, Norman-Bel Geddes, Raymond O'Neil, Irving Pichel, Thomas Wood Stevens, Lee Simonson, Rollo Peters, Kenneth Macgowan, Frederic McConnell—these men who have been leaders in our own insurgent movement, besides having vision and perseverance and belief in America, have known intimately the work and the ideas of the chief artists of the European stage. Not one of these local leaders but acknowledges his debt to Gordon Craig, takes off his hat to Stanislavsky, calls Copeau brother, and remembers with a thrill the visit of the Irish Players.

The point is that in Europe there already exist a number of playhouses, so removed from the commercial theater, by ideals and organization, as to merit the distinctive title "art theaters"; and to us in our beginnings, in our gropings, and in our growing period, there are many fruitful lessons to be learned from their experience, their repertories, their methods of organization. There is, too, a heartening parallel in that they originally developed out of a period of discontent, of revolt against the business theater, of amateur enthusiasm, exactly like that existing in America to-day.

From the artist's standpoint the "regular" European theaters of thirty or forty years ago seemed almost as hopeless, indeed, as did our American business theaters of ten or fifteen years back. The cause was not so clearly or exclusively a deadening commercialism, but rather a stultifying traditionalism, a slavish adherence to conventions that had little to do with the life of the time. The protests of Antoine in France, of the rebels in Germany from Brahm to Fuchs, and of Gordon Craig in England and throughout Europe, when re-read sound remarkably like those of our own "radicals" of the last fifteen years. Dramatic production, while never quite so dominated by business considerations, was quite as stereotyped as on this side of the Atlantic. In short, the conservatives, the anti-progressives, held the theaters; and the artist-thinkers, the forward-looking workers, could renounce their better selves, or turn to other arts—or revolt in such small ways as their means and an indifferent public would permit.

I

The revolt started with the *Théâtre Libre* movement. How far that development differed in ideals from the art theater movement has not been sufficiently emphasized in the past. Its ultimate aims were quite foreign to what is essentially implied in the later development. But it was negatively very important, for it cleared away a lot of the old superstitions of the stage and opened the playhouse to innovators and amateurs.

It was in 1887 that André Antoine, a clerk in the gas company at Paris, founded the *Théâtre Libre.* For nearly a decade he courageously produced there, with the unqualified approval of a small group, and with the bitterest censure of the conservative critics and public, the most radical compositions of naturalistic and realistic writers. Then he founded the *Théâtre Antoine*, where he continued the naturalistic tradition, but without the worst excesses of the earlier venture. The movement spread to Germany with the foundation of the *Freie Bühne* at Berlin in 1889, with Otto Brahm as Director; and in 1891 J. T. Grein established the Independent Theater in London.

All these theaters bore the earmarks of a definite movement. All were private or subscription ventures—merely a way of evading censorship. All announced their object as rebellion against the monopolistic and anti-libertarian commercial theater and the tradition-bound official theater. All were definitely dedicated to naturalism or realism as an art standard.

In France the movement was narrower than in Germany and England. Although some plays of Ibsen and others of the Northern dramatists were introduced, French drama was produced almost exclusively. Perhaps because of this provincial limitation there developed no easily detected French school or movement to carry on the impetus created by Antoine's group, so that there was a long sterile period between the experiments of Antoine and those of Copeau.

In Germany the *Freie Bühne* was more truly a free theater in the international sense, and it had the widest effect upon the regular playhouses. Its work, indeed, was so well done that the grip of traditionalism was largely broken in Germany by the end of the century. The original revolutionary playhouse went out of existence, but theaters throughout Germany had then been opened to the new drama, and the way had been cleared for the coming of new ideas of production and the creation of many living progressive stages.

In England the movement culminated in the development of an exceedingly important group of realistic-intellectual dramatists: Shaw, Barker, Galsworthy, and a half dozen lesser writers. But, as in France, the achievement was not far-reaching. The institution of the theater as a whole was very little changed. The playwright with new ideas still finds himself an outsider, and such contributions as England has made to an art theater technique can be summed up in the independent pioneering of the exiled Gordon Craig, such short-lived experiments as Granville Barker's brief "seasons" as director, and the more permanent but less inspired repertory theater ventures in the provinces.

Finally the naturalistic development flowered most brilliantly in the achievement of the Moscow Art

Theater, where realistic works took on a value almost unknown or extremely rare elsewhere, through extraordinary sympathy, cleverness and simplicity in the acting. This theater also carried over from the *Théâtre Libre* period into the post-realistic period, and is so important in later history that I shall give considerable space to it a few pages later.

It is probable that the whole realistic movement in the theater has been vastly over-rated as a positive contribution to dramatic art. Its negative value as paving the way for the next phase is incalculable at this early time; and its social value as restoring a healthy relationship between the theater and contemporary life is immense. But its final achievement, its contribution to the development of a distinctive modern art of the theater, has been slight even as compared with the as-yet-immature "art theater movement." The naturalists and more extreme realists, in the desire to limit themselves to showing a segment of life, or to proving a thesis, missed something of the theatrical, the spiritual, the imaginative, the eternal. At worst, their plays are displeasing, vulgar, and even immoral and disgusting; at best they are narrowed down to an unimaginative corner of art-expression.

The *Théâtre Libre* movement, then, insofar as it concerns the present study, had only these effects: it demolished superstitions regarding professionalism, opened the theater to new types of drama, substituted a natural (if usually uninspired) sort of acting for the old pompous artificiality and conventionality, and proved that a simple style-less setting or no setting at all is better than the old crassly artificial or consciously spectacular background. For the really constructive phase that followed, for the beginnings of the theater to be built in the clearing thus made, one must go back to an independent impulse—to the Craig-Appia-Reinhardt movement, if one may so name it from the most notable three artists concerned.

II

The most important figure in the new theater, because most inspiring and most typical of the artist to come, is Gordon Craig. He was fitted by both heredity and early training to take a place in the accepted theater. But during his brief experience there he chafed under its limitations and restraints, and finally broke away entirely, to become the ablest and most active crusader for a new art of the theater—the greatest outsider of them all.

Craig pointed out first the lack of art in the existing playhouse, charging that the men of the theater were purveying a sort of play based on a false conception of dramatic ideals. While castigating the bunglers in the commercial theater, he protested against the playhouse being taken over by either the literary artists or the easel painters. He also turned his guns on another set of reformers, being always an unsparing critic of realism, and never missing an opportunity to call for dramatic imaginativeness and poetry to help save the stage.

After his destructive criticism came a constructive

one in the form of a plea for artists of vision in the theater. The usual production, he rightfully argued, is not a work of art at all, because it lacks that binding spiritual quality, that unity of feeling, which can be achieved only through the creative effort of an artist. The performance is a thing of scattered effect depending upon chance association of playwright, actor, scene-painter, electrician, carpenter, and stage-manager. If there is one brain supervising all, it is that of a businessman, or actor, incapable of visualizing the production in imaginative form, and necessarily delegating bits of control to this and that assistant. Craig therefore called for the training of a new race of theater artists, of creative producers who would be able to impart a theatrical unity to every production they brought to the stage.

Through all the years since he promulgated the artist-director theory, Gordon Craig has sought passionately the methods by which the artist could obtain unity of mood in the theater, and he has re-tested every element of stage craftsmanship in relation to a unifying principle. He did more than any other artist to reform stage setting, combating on the one hand the ridiculous artificiality and the spectacular vulgarity of the old style scene, and on the other the photographic perfection and meticulous appeal of the naturalistic method. He sought to substitute suggestion in place of imitation, simplicity in place of elaboration, expressiveness in place of showiness; and always he insisted upon a definite spiritual or emotional relationship between the background and the action. He insisted that current ideals of acting must change: that the actor must subordinate his personality and become a willing part of a larger design, obedient to the will of the artist-director, and that the pernicious star system must be destroyed. He attached a new value to movement on the stage, pointing out the emotional effectiveness of figures moving in design, of shifting light and shadow, of changing pattern of colour. And finally he pointed out that the stage production, which started out to be an art appealing to the eye—theater means "a place for seeing"—had become merely a platform for the recitation of words appealing through the ear to the intellect and emotions. He made his plea for a new art of the theater which would be not merely mentally or emotionally stirring, but satisfying through typical *theatrical* appeal. In these things he laid down foundation principles for the whole art theater movement.

An artist equally original, but more elusive, is Adolphe Appia. He has never had the same influence, because he failed to get his ideas before the world in concrete form; and in England and America his influence has been slight because there has never been a translation, or even adequate interpretation, of his important books. Very early in his career, while applying his experiments exclusively to opera, he arrived at certain conclusions which have come to be basic principles of the new race of theater artists: that the realistic and painted-perspective modes of stage setting are impossible artistically; that there must be unity of play, setting and action; that the actor is the factor to be emphasized within this unity—that he and not a trick of staging must be the center of the picture; and finally, that lighting can be largely utilized as the uniting force, binding together all the elements of the production, by providing an all-pervading spiritual atmosphere. The emphasis on the value of light, and the insistence that the lighting must be definitely designed to further dramatic meaning, is Appia's most distinctive contribution to the new staging.

From these two, Craig and Appia, the art theater movement may be considered to start. Of those who helped shape it in Europe, of those who added to the mass of theory, or proved or disproved this or that theory in practice, I shall say little except as they happen to be concerned in five playhouses: the Munich Art Theater, the Moscow Art Theater, Max Reinhardt's *Deutsches Theater*, the Abbey Theater in Dublin and the *Théâtre du Vieux Colombier*. I am conscious that this is an arbitrary choice; but I think that these offer in their beginnings and development the nearest parallels to our conditions in America, and in their achievement are the most suggestive of ways in which we are likely to grow.

To indicate the breadth of the new spirit, however, it is well to remember that France claimed one of the first experiments in the new field, in the establishment of the *Théâtre de l'Œuvre* in 1893 as a sort of artists' protest against naturalism and that Jacques Rouché made sincere efforts to realize the synthetic art theater ideal at his *Théâtre des Arts* in Paris. But these and the English ventures are less important than those chosen for more extended description. I am leaving out also all description of the Volksbühne in Berlin, because it is most interesting in the organizational aspect, and I shall have much to say about it in a later chapter.

III

The famous Moscow Art Theater was founded under circumstances strikingly like those surrounding the beginnings of the most important little theaters in this country. The group originating the venture was more amateur than professional, and its object was definitely to explore regions untouched by the regular theaters. It was distinctly a reform theater, and like most of its kind it utilized at first amateur actors and students, and sought its designers in the fields of the other arts.

After renouncing the ideals of the commercial theater, and its methods of playwriting, acting and stage setting, it turned first to the exploration and exploitation of realism. It sought to create the illusion of life by detailed imitation. The theater was thus immediately rid of the old artificiality of acting, and the faultiness of current modes of staging was exposed. But naturalism and uninspired realism soon proved unequal to the demands of a typical art theater organization. Or perhaps more correctly it may be said that a group of theater artists of the ability of Stanislavsky's company were able by sincerity, sympathetic interpretation and supremely clever characterization to lift the best realistic plays to a new significance; and

The cottage scene in *The Blue Bird* as produced at the Moscow Art Theater. From a sketch by V. E. Yegoroff. (From Jacques Rouché's *L'Art theatrale moderne.*)

even then were not content until they had come to an unexampled proficiency in staging Shakespeare, Maeterlinck and the Greeks in some newer "style." At any rate those many progressives who have been seeking a way out of realist-domination in the world theater, have stood speechless at the achievement of a new effectiveness, a new theatrical intensity, in the plays of Tchehoff and Gorky as performed by this company, and have granted that this accomplishment, together with outstanding productions like the famous *Blue Bird* and *Hamlet*, warranted the claim that during the first two decades of the Twentieth Century the Moscow Art Theater was the "world's first theater"—i. e., the finest of all art theaters.

Anyone who reads Stanislavsky's *My Life in Art* will feel above all else the way in which his mind constantly grew in experiment, changing conditions of life and the theater, in contact with his own associates and the foremost creative artists of Europe. Constant search, spiritual breadth, the wonder of new discovery, these keep pace with his deep love of the theater and his desire for expression. And through it all there is growing the sense of the importance of a theatrical unity, a spiritual unity, a binding force in production, which more than anything else has become the distinctive mark of art theater activity. Whether in the original field of realism, or in the search for the imaginative, the symbolic, the lyrical, there was constantly the effort to find a method that would be at once a simplification, an intensification and an enrichment of the play-text—a creative contribution on the part of actors, director, and designer working in accord.

There are those who will say that the contribution of the Moscow Art Theater is wholly within the naturalistic period, that it is simply the highest expression of a form of art that is now fast becoming outmoded. Others find a wedding of realistic and symbolistic or idealistic. Ten years ago I could write in this connection: "It may well be that the drama of the future lies in a compromise between these two ideals, or rather in a fusing of the intense life-truth [whatever that may be!] of the one with the spiritualizing idealism of the other. It may be, indeed, that the Moscow Art Theater has made its greatest contribution to modern art through its experiments in search of an enlightened and spiritualized realism." Well, well, that may conceivably be; I probably had a real glimmer of something about the intensity of realism captured with anti-realistic, purely theatrical means. But it is a little early for anyone still living to get sufficient perspective to talk intelligently about that.

The points which should most interest American progressives are these: A non-star organization was brought into being, in which the actors studied and worked intelligently and harmoniously together, while always obedient to an enlightened artist-director. The theater is efficiently administered as a business venture, but businessmen have nothing to say about types of play or methods of staging, and the project is not subject to shifting this way or that for the sake of profits. The administration and ownership are in the hands of men of high ideals and artists of broad insight. There is a body of actors who are willing (and can afford) to accept a moderate wage because they love their work and enjoy permanent employment. There is a complex and delicate adjustment of duties between a general administrative department (the Direction) and a production department (the Council) that chooses plays, and plans and supervises productions.* While preserving an experimental ideal, the theater has arrived at an amazing perfection of performance. It has developed artists who have gone out to help revolutionize theaters formerly devoted to commercial ideas. And finally it has refused to be satisfied with a building and equipment inadequate to the requirements of a broadly artistic type of production; the architecture is restful, and the mechanical features fairly adequate.

In regard to the last point, the Munich Art Theater has often been held up as a model architecturally, and I wish to emphasize here certain relationships between such a building and the development of the new art of the theater. Our American theaters are notoriously

* Oliver Sayler, who first gave Americans extended accounts of the Moscow Art Theater and press-agented the company's visits to this country, tells me that there has been a recent re-organization, under which a great deal of power has been concentrated in the hands of Nyemirovitch-Dantchenko, President of "the Direction." This does not mean that control is being given to the "business" element in the theater—for Dantchenko is no less the visionary artist than is Stanislavsky, having been writer, dramatist, teacher and amateur stage director before joining with Stanislavsky in the founding of the Moscow Art Theater. The change is merely one more indication that in an institutional theater there must be centralized, almost autocratic control, if there is to be life.

lacking in atmosphere, and it is doubtful whether the insurgent movement in this country will not lag until we have a group of playhouses that are in harmony with the spirit of dramatic art at its best. Many visitors to the Munich Art Theater, accustomed to American and English theaters, or to French ornateness, have testified to the remarkable sense of restfulness experienced upon entering the auditorium. In such an atmosphere the spectator is immediately put into a state of receptivity, and the producer's battle to create a single harmonious impression is already partially won. This sympathetic sort of architecture, no less than equipment of the most modern type, is necessary to a full realization of the new ideal.

But the Munich Art Theater as an institution was important for more reasons than appear in its architectural form—though that may be taken as symbolic of an all-pervading artistic thoroughness. Its search, to quote Huntly Carter, was for "simplification, synthesis, rhythm and beauty"—and such aims alone set it apart from the great mass of theaters. It sought to "preserve the unity of the action of the drama in cooperation with sound, color, motion." One limitation should be noted: the stage was built very shallow, because the directors were concerned in the beginning with a too narrow conception of the new art of staging—that of the "relief-theater." The pioneer work accomplished there, nevertheless, was exceedingly valuable, in both its practical and its inspirational aspects.

The impulse for its founding came from without the old theater, and it has consistently utilized the talents of inspired outsiders. It immediately discarded all the old paraphernalia of the stage, and set out to prove that conventionalized settings, aided by simplicity, breadth and suggestion, could create illusion more satisfyingly than the most elaborate imitations in the naturalistic method. It stood for a synthesis of forces on the stage, but with the emphasis on the actors, who, besides carrying the story, supplied through designed movement that decorative quality which was formerly supposed to reside in the setting alone. The efficacy of the production purely theatrically, the art value as distinguished from the mere dramatic value or acting value or spectacular value, was discovered to be dependent upon *style*, a reflection of the individual genius of the artists concerned in the staging. And finally, while it remained typically a theater of the artists, it was not thereby condemned to business mismanagement.

While it is right that the Americans (and English) should go to Craig for the larger conceptions of modern theater art, and particularly for the urge to creativeness—no one could talk to the man or read his books without being stimulated, even inflamed, to get up and do something about the stage—it is to another that they must turn to learn the "practical" values of something approaching art theater standards of production. Stanislavsky and his company have acknowledged their debt to Gordon Craig, and even took him to Moscow to design their *Hamlet* production; and Fuchs was enormously in his debt. But the man who profited most by Craig's ideas, who took them up and acclimated them to a practical (and money-power) world was Max Reinhardt. Expediency tempered his enthusiasm for the new ideas of staging—particularly that typically Craigesque idea that art is arrived at by long contemplation and extended and painstaking experiment and training before anything is shown to the public. Reinhardt saw a vision of a play in more or less the new "form"; and he went after it, in the usual way, and carried it through to presentation. He doubtless blundered often, as one must who uses the tools at hand and does his experimenting more or less publicly. But he blundered through to the best compromise success that any artist-director of the post-naturalistic period has achieved. His *Deutsches Theater* in Berlin has been cited many times as the best example of a "practical art theater." Certainly it went forward in a businesslike way while subsisting on dramatic fare which the "regular" theaters considered very special. Many managers will tell you that the reason we have not such theaters in America is that no such enlightened audience exists here as that of the German capital. It was therefore with special delight that I recently encountered a paragraph in an article on Reinhardt to the effect that one of the chief obstacles he had to overcome before establishing the *Deutsches Theater* was the insistence of his friends that in Berlin audiences did not exist for such a playhouse. In Moscow and Paris, perhaps, or even in Vienna, but certainly not in Berlin!

In America, of course, the trouble lies in the lack of a director like Max Reinhardt, who combines business genius with a comprehensive knowledge of the art of the theater. Such a director would immediately find the means to build in New York a theater embodying the German architectural ideal—there is no dodging the fact that it is the best in the world to-day—and in it he would present a series of plays clearly artistic in general tone, and yet commercially successful. He would do this because he would be an opportunist, with an eye to his public. That is, he would vary his experiments and his productions of limited appeal with others that leaned toward the tried and accepted formulas; and he would add enough of sensationalism to be sure of sufficient audiences. Of course the resultant theater would not be so typical an expression of the movement as would a playhouse modeled after the Moscow Art Theater. It would be a compromise; but a compromise like the *Deutsches Theater* would be considerably better than anything now existing in New York. Consider what it would mean, for instance, to have an established playhouse where Shakespeare, Molière, Goethe, Schiller, Shaw, Wilde, Ibsen, Tolstoy, Schnitzler and every important contemporary native dramatist took turns at appearing, all presented under a director with a genius for finding and utilizing the best actors and the best designers in the country. Not a Craig theater or a Stanislavsky theater; but a mighty interesting improvement over our business theaters, and infinitely broader than any of our institutional theaters as yet.

If Max Reinhardt has compromised with the older theater and with the public, he nevertheless has made the *Deutsches Theater* and its annex, the *Kammerspiele*, one of the most notable dramatic centers in the world, and in many ways a model for progressives everywhere. His stages are as completely equipped according to standards of the new stagecraft as any others in Europe, and in staging and choice of plays he has been ready to accept the newest ideas at least for trial. He has drawn many of the leading German designers and painters to the stage, if not with uniformly satisfying results, still with broadening and gratifying effect upon both the theater and the artists concerned. The acting of his company is one more assurance that the star system belongs to a lower type of production, and that only with intelligent ensemble acting can the best be accomplished. And if some of his productions overshoot the mark, there still is evidence in the success of most of them that the indispensable factor is thoroughness, unity attained through one director's vision.

Perhaps the most independent theater of modern times is the *Théâtre du Vieux Colombier* of Jacques Copeau in Paris. To be sure, it recently closed its doors, but we all hope it is only for a year's holiday, for recreation of the spirit and to gain a new perspective—as our own Neighborhood and Provincetown Playhouses closed for the season 1922–23, only to reopen with new energy, renewed vision.

Copeau's venture was born out of what he has illuminatingly termed *indignation.* The stupidity, the shallowness, the falsity of the offerings of the boulevard playhouses made this lover of the theater very weary and very indignant. For years he worked over the idea of beginning at the beginning of dramatic art and creating a new stage in Paris. His plan evolved as part of a broader cultural movement in France, the literary and artistic development that centered around the *Nouvelle Revue Française*. He also derived somewhat from Gordon Craig and Adolphe Appia, and was influenced by a great admiration for Synge and the Irish Players. But no theater ever grew out of one man's vision and faith more than did the *Vieux Colombier*.

Copeau before he became the director of a theater and an actor was a literary man. All through his protests, his experiments and his achievement there is apparent the attitude of one who sees the written script as the heart of dramatic production. He minimized scenic effect, returning to what is the nearest modern approach to the bare platform, the simple Elizabethan stage. He has been unalterably opposed to the rule of the decorators in the theater. He puts emphasis where it belongs, on the actors, but first he makes sure that his actors have lived with the dramatist's text, have understood it, felt it, loved it.

In 1913 Copeau published a pamphlet of protest and promise, under the title *Un Essai de Rénovation Dramatique*, which is one of the most inspiriting documents of the new movement. "Rénovation" should be translated, perhaps, as revivification rather than merely renovation. For the note of it goes deep. Go back to the sources, start on new foundation, create afresh. Avoid alike the methods and means of the existing commercial-official theater, and the theories for reforming it. Remember only that the theater may be a place for beauty, and build slowly, contemplatively, simply toward that. In Paris Copeau adapted his little theater from a hall, copied its chief architectural features at the Garrick Theater in New York and spent two seasons there during the war, and in 1920 opened a small playhouse nearer his ideal in Paris.

There are many lessons for America, of course, in Copeau's accomplishment. The repertory system and the breadth of the repertory. And a thorough craftsmanship. No one ever went at the work of knowing his tools and using them honestly, joyfully, skillfully, with more love than did this poet-actor-producer. But perhaps chief among the facts that our hasty enthusiasts over here should ponder is this: Copeau before he showed his first play took his little company away to the country and studied through a whole summer with them; he made a virtue of his lack of great means, building an economical stage and resisting every temptation to "spread"; and never once in a decade of producing has he tried to meet the "competition" of the commercial theater. Waldo Frank, in a brochure published while Copeau had his company in New York, called "The Art of the Vieux Colombier," wrote as follows about this avoidance of entanglement with the business theater: "Consider what the *Vieux Colombier* was, in relation to the world. It was no reaction from the commercial theater upon that theater's plane; it was a lifting up of the theater upon another plane: or rather, the invasion of another plane upon the theater. And it was very specially a revolt from all those artistic hindrances and falsities that come with a great financial burden. The *Vieux Colombier* had vowed to do without the triumphs of the market-place in order to be without its jurisdiction. It moved outside the vicious circle of material competition and material success."

Read that, O Theater Guild and Actors' Theater, and take heed! The directorate of the Guild has recently felt constrained to justify in print its financial and material success, and with some reason. It strikes me at the moment that what I wrote a few pages back and eight years ago about Reinhardt and compromise was fairly close to the Guild formula: if he came to New York, "he would vary his experiments and his productions of limited appeal with others that leaned toward the tried and accepted formulas; and he would add enough of sensationalism to be sure of sufficient audiences." The program fits the Guild record too exactly for comfort if one has in mind anything like Copeau's artistic integrity and independence. The Actors' Theater, on the other hand, has slipped not so much in the matter of accepted formulas or sensationalism as in disregard for the deeper economic laws of existence for institutional theaters: when it had its two financial successes this year—both with plays of sterling worth in their realistic-intellectual field—it abandoned its subscribers mid-season to enjoy the material rewards of long runs. It is not a permanent defection, but a disquieting sign of lack of purpose and lack of belief in something better than Broadway.

The experience and achievement of one other theater are peculiarly suggestive when examined beside the American problem—not so much, perhaps, in relation to the ultimate American art theater, and certainly not in relation to New York, but as a guide and encouragement in our beginnings. The Abbey Theater in Dublin, the theater of the Irish Players, was founded and has continued as an expression of the amateur spirit. Its first phase was "The Irish Literary Theater," an ephemeral institution brought into being by three literary artists, Edward Martyn, W. B. Yeats and George Moore. After the Literary Theater's short career closed, its ideals were taken up, broadened and carried on by the Irish National Theater, to which the chief new contribution was brought by another theorist, in the shape of a simplified, distinguished mode of acting. A group of native amateur actors under the direction of an inspired leader began that exciting adventure which has carried the name of the Irish Players through all the dramatic world. Native playwrights, stimulated to effort by the opportunity of seeing their plays sympathetically and intelligently produced, wrote dramas of not only local but universal appeal. Other new impulses were added, the most important perhaps being that of Gordon Craig's simplified methods of staging—for that added reform of scene to reform of playwriting and acting. And so there came into being an Irish theater in which the amateur spirit lived under professional organization, a theater in which beauty and sincerity were guiding principles.

The economic history of the Irish players also holds a lesson for the American theater. The Dublin project struggled along at first in rented halls and without adequate stage facilities; but at a critical time a woman of wealth recognized the merit of the workers, remodeled a theater, offered it rent-free for six years, and provided a small subsidy. It reminds us that most of the really fruitful art schemes find outside financial aid in the years of struggle, and that American little theaters must find several wealthy people with Miss Horniman's insight and generous appreciation before the impulse toward an art theater can find full expression.

The total effect of the art theaters on the general theatrical situation in Europe is interesting, although it offers no direct parallel to conditions in America. In Germany the whole country has grown with the movement, and it is possible to find in State and commercial theaters frequent productions approximating art theater ideals. Certainly in no other country are there so many theaters with broad repertories, with modern ideals and means of production, and with progressive artist-directors in charge. The Germans had no monopolistic, utterly commercialized institution to fight against, and they already had many endowed playhouses. Their problem was merely to increase the already large number of experienced artist-directors, and gradually to reorganize their theaters with these men in charge.

France too has its endowed state and municipal theaters, but it has profited less by the achievement of the art-theater groups. The French tradition in acting, French preoccupation with French variations on French themes in playwriting, French dislike for German reform ideas in plays, setting or theater architecture—all these have combined to offer effective resistance to the "new ideas" in Paris theaters. Copeau and his lieutenant Jouvet are the foremost and only important world-figures from our present viewpoint. The rest is of an earlier time.

In England the continental art theaters have had unmistakable influence on the development of a group of repertory theaters in the provinces—the most hopeful sign in what would otherwise appear a none too active field. These repertory theaters not only are keeping alive the best out of the realistic movement, but are making some progress toward the art theater's synthetic methods of production. They await, I think, the coming of a race of inspired artist-directors. Perhaps Barry V. Jackson of the Birmingham Repertory Theater should be cited as example, for his pioneering—although his service has been locally significant rather than nationally or internationally. Nugent Monck, with his amateur Norwich Players, has made a real contribution through experiment in producing the classics on a stage modeled after those of pre-Restoration times (the debt going back in part to that unique student-producer, William Poel); and at the other extreme Nigel Playfair has done some unusual professional productions, fully stylized, at the

Lyric Theater, Hammersmith. The Everyman Theater at Hampstead, under the direction of Norman Macdermott, has also been a sign of new life stirring. But in general London lags; since Craig's leaving and Barker's lapse to inactivity, England has shown only these few too timid thrusts toward the established creative theater, toward the crystallization of individualistic vision. For the most part, the country seems satisfied with the fare it finds in its older conservative theater, varied with brief Sunday excursions to something inherited from the *Freie Bühne* age, as purveyed by the Stage Society. Theatrical leadership of the English-speaking world has shifted to New York.

CHAPTER III

THE COMING OF THE ART THEATER: AMERICA

New York as leader. It is leadership by energy, promise, extraordinarily vital beginnings, rather than achievement in terms of long-established institutional theaters and artist-giants as in Moscow, Berlin, Dresden, Munich, Prague. There is no theater in New York with the individuality of the *Vieux Colombier*, despite the example of Copeau's transplanted stage and company at the Garrick Theater through two seasons. The Cleveland Playhouse comes nearer to that distinctiveness, and Maurice Browne achieved it in a measure at the Chicago Little Theater. Nor is there a Volksbühne, or a theater approaching the established standards of Jessner at the State Theater in Berlin, or of Linnebach at Dresden. But in New York there are theaters with a character of their own—the Neighborhood Playhouse and the Provincetown Playhouse—and there are organizations that have traveled a long way on the road toward established professional art theater production.

In Europe the revolt against the established theater has as often as not grown out of the vision and determination of amateurs, artists, outsiders: Copeau, the writer, Stanislavsky, the amateur actor and dilettante, Antoine, the gas company clerk, Shaw, the critic; but there have been great figures rising out of professionalism, too: Gordon Craig, himself an actor and the son of Ellen Terry; Reinhardt, who seems never to have lived or worked outside a playhouse. But the secessionists from the regular theater in America are few. A business despotism begets no artistic rebels, and so almost the complete story here is about outsiders. It remained for college groups, dilettante artists, decorators, architects, amateur actors, to divine the universal significance of the Craig-Appia-Reinhardt phenomenon, and to begin in their inexperienced way the building of a new theater.

I

There are those who will tell you that the endowed professional art theater was long ago tried in America and failed—referring, of course, to the New Theater. In the first place that institution was not endowed. If it had been, the building would still be given up to experimenting with art, instead of being dedicated as it is now to any old spectacle or musical show that can pay the rent. In the second place the director of the New Theater venture, Winthrop Ames, although he stands as perhaps the most enlightened and one of the most able of the Broadway managers, has never quite seen the new institutional theater as Stanislavsky or Copeau sees it. He was not the typical artist-director, although he is much more the artist than the great majority of his fellows among the producing managers. In certain directions he did wonders at the New Theater, particularly in the building up of a group of actors individually capable but devoted to the ensemble ideal—and his example will prove of value later; but he failed to coördinate the departments of staging to the extent of obtaining the unity of impression so typical of art theater work. Moreover, he was subject to a governing board which was not even theatrical-minded, and he was victim of a rigid system that demanded a new play every third week. But the most important cause of the New Theater's failure to establish itself as an integral part of American art life lay in the fact that it tried to begin at the top, in imitation of the most pretentious European repertory theaters. It was never a native theater, with roots in American life and with native experience behind it. If we ever have in America a successful institution of the aristocratic sort that the New Theater was intended to be, it will come after the democratic, native art theater has been established as a part of American cultural life.

II

The story of the native little theaters can be carried back some twenty years. But the period 1911–12 seems the proper starting-point for an essay on the institutional theater of the particular sort I have sketched. Three significant organizations, the Wisconsin Dramatic Society (later the Wisconsin Players), the Toy Theater in Boston, and the Chicago Little Theater all came to life in those two seasons. The Toy Theater, after being a valuable center of experiment under the direction of Mrs. Lyman Gale, went out of existence in 1916, when its ambitions outgrew its wisdom. The Wisconsin Players continue, but have failed to mature out of the experimental class, although they have done fine pioneering work, particularly in the matter of early opening a new channel of expression for the native playwright. The Chicago Little Theater, like the Toy, went out of existence after five years of producing; but its service was so great as example, its accomplishment so distinctive, that it is likely to be remembered as the most significant adventure in the field of the art theater in America during the first twenty years of the Twentieth Century. Most important of all, it set a standard to attain, in play choice and in presentation; and it introduced new and revolutionary methods of staging. It closed finally in 1917, passed into history, but had created an impetus that is still felt wherever the younger groups of artists and organizers are gathering to plot new theatrical ventures. Outstanding in a different way, but less distinctive artistically, was the Arts and Crafts Theater in Detroit. Its special claim to attention, perhaps, lay in its success in proving that the little theater could, even in wartime, pay its way economically, if it compromised somewhat with public taste in play selection. It had personality, too, and it established a high standard of presentation. But it also came to an end, for reasons that will be outlined in a later chapter.

III

The Neighborhood Playhouse in New York grew

out of native conditions and has fulfilled its destiny more flourishingly than any other of our institutional theaters. And yet it is likely to be an art theater only second, and a social-experiment theater first through all its life. And it is not likely to be at all a broad repertory institution with a rich and varied list of plays constantly available for revival. The Neighborhood Playhouse was opened in 1915. The building represents as near an ideal plant as any little theater group is likely to own. It is administered by directors who came to the community, the Jewish East Side, because they recognized that it was rich in dramatic talent and ripe for self-expression in a theater.

The organization originally grew out of a "settlement," but it is much more than a branch of a social-work society. It has its own more or less permanent company, it has financial backing, it has an ideal stage and working plant, and it has found its own audience. Fortunately it is content not to want to play in competition with Broadway, and equally content to remain the sort of theater that "Neighborhood" implies, rather than the kind of pretentious art institution that the "New Theater" aspired to be. Its plays are as often as not chosen with an eye to the social problems involved in the plots, or because there is opportunity to try out something that no other theater in America cared to take a chance on. The group has perfectly lived up to a line in its opening announcement: "By the variety of its program, the Playhouse aims to appeal to a public of diverse tastes, interests and ages,

The Neighborhood Playhouse. One of the pioneer institutional theaters in New York, and home of one of the very few permanent acting companies in America. (H. C. Ingalls and F. B. Hoffman, Jr., Architects.)

and in this way to share in the life of the Neighborhood." The staging of plays, too, shows a variable merit. Occasionally a production is so fine that audiences flock down to Grand Street from uptown, until finally the Playhouse directors have to wrench the successful play out of the program to continue the regular subscription series—a sacrifice unfailingly made, to the end that the larger permanent scheme may persist.

As to serving all New York as an art theater, the Neighborhood Playhouse's function will thus be limited: theatergoers on the lookout for the best will be drawn down to Grand Street two or three times a year. The rest of the time they will stay away with the knowledge that the playhouse is fulfilling its other destiny of giving the East Side a variety of things and a means to self-expression.

IV

The Provincetown Players are at the other extreme. Service to art has been their one reason for being. At first it was the segregated and incomplete art of the playwright. In 1915 the group organized at Provincetown, Massachusetts, the summer home of many Greenwich Village artists and writers. Its one purpose at first was to provide a stage for the new American dramatist who could find no other outlet for really original work—a home for creative imagination in the native theater. From 1916 to 1922 the Provincetown Playhouse in New York, a cramped little stage and a bare and unattractive room of an auditorium, functioned as a laboratory for new plays by known and unknown authors. It made many of its own playwrights, out of writers in other fields; and it came to be known as "the Playwrights' Theater." It gave Eugene O'Neill his chance to prove himself; and O'Neill has been half the organization ever since. Next in importance there was Susan Glaspell. And after her a remarkable list of authors who were less instrumental in developing the organization, but of note as both writers and effective insurgents: Alfred Kreymborg, Edna St. Vincent Millay, Maxwell Bodenheim, Floyd Dell, Harry Kemp, Djuna Barnes. As director there was George Cram Cook. It was clearly a theater of the radicals; more so than the Washington Square Players or the Neighborhood or any of the Western groups. Radicalism at the moment meant deeper realism than Broadway audiences were ready to face—although Kreymborg and Miss Millay did something to balance the ultra-realists. At any rate, here was native insurgency at its best: a theater that did more than any other to open the channel of creative playwriting. A theater that staged its offerings only passably well, sometimes very crudely, but never with the false glamour of typical Broadway staging. A true step, in the beginning, toward a native creative stage.

In 1922–23 the Provincetown Playhouse was closed. The old group had served its purpose, and decided there should be an interim to restudy conditions and gain new strength. Two years ago a reorganization put the project into the hands of three directors, each in some way a pioneer in the struggle toward a new theater, and only one a member of the old group: Eugene O'Neill, Robert Edmond Jones and Kenneth Macgowan; playwright, artist, critic. The achievement in the two years since has been extremely uneven if judged by an art theater standard of acting. Some things have been so badly done that the need for better direction has shrieked aloud. But in general the group marches toward its goal with increasing surety—as was to be expected under such guidance *and* with O'Neill's plays always handy to fill a gap or replenish the treasury. Full reliance on American authors gave way to the idea of experiment in new methods of staging, and experiment in importing the latest plays of European radicals. The native author has had his place too: Stark Young, Edmund Wilson Jr., Hatcher Hughes. These are not so radical as those of the earlier days, but plenty far away from the theater of commerce. Along with these, Strindberg, Vildrac, Hasenclever. And stylized revivals of *Fashion* and *Patience*.

The Provincetowners have found many progressives as well as conservatives ready to criticize their record in these two years of struggle to re-find themselves. But they at least have had courage and they have presented an amazing variety of drama. They have failed to build anything like an adequate acting machine, their professionals being hardly at all of the first rank, and no director having emerged with genius to train them into an ensemble. During the season just closing they have had two theaters constantly open—the tiny Provincetown and the larger Greenwich Village Theater—and have also sent companies uptown when the demand (for O'Neill) warranted. It is announced that next year the functions of the two home playhouses will be more distinct than heretofore, the Provincetown devoting itself to frank experiment, and the Greenwich Village to more recognized plays and a more adequate professional standard of production. So far the organization has given the impression of experimenting all over the place, hit or miss—and missing as often as it hit. If it can keep up to its own best standard in one house, with a permanent company, *there* will be one of the art theaters we are seeking.

V

The same year that saw the opening of the Neighborhood Playhouse and the founding of the Provincetown Players witnessed the beginnings of another very important venture. Again it was artists, writers and talkers of Greenwich Village who were ripe for rebellion against conditions in the commercial theater, determined to present plays that would not otherwise be seen on the American stage, and to give the creative American playwright his chance. The Washington Square Players organized, took the little Bandbox Theater way uptown, and immediately found audiences for the "special" things they were interested in presenting. After two seasons in the side-street theater, they moved down to one of the smaller Broadway houses. It is difficult to say whether it was this unwise move into competition with the commercial producers, before the group was thoroughly professionalized (in the better sense, of knowing their craft thoroughly), or the vicissitudes of the war, that put them out of existence. At any rate, halfway through their second season in the new home, they found further going impossible. But they had established something novel in New York, had presented many brilliant plays, among others less brilliant, and had tried the experiment of the new spirit functioning through more or less professional casts. They had displayed that courage, that independent judgment and that disregard for dead but treasured conventions which were so essential to a healthy insurgency at that time. They had also trained in the ways of the progressive theater several artists and executives who were to loom large in the next important attempt to establish an art theater in New York, the Theater Guild.

The Theater Guild, be it said at once, is America's nearest approach to an established repertory art theater. It is firmly anchored in the community, has its own home, and produces plays that are far above the commercial theater standard. If it only approximates the true type as yet, that is because it has failed to develop a resident company of actors or an inspired artist-director, and has shunned the true repertory system of repeated revivals. It has its firm material foundation and these other things will come.

The Guild was organized in the Spring of 1919. The new group was generously indebted to the old

Washington Square Players, and three of the directing board had been among the organizers of the earlier project. But equally important was the new blood that came in: Rollo Peters, who was initiator, and became the first director of the Guild; and Helen Freeman and Augustin Duncan, who brought a wholesome note of professionalism to the scheme. The first productions of the new organization, due to the better balance of the group, showed a far firmer grasp on the problems of acting and staging than had the Washington Square productions—less of the carelessly amateurish. And yet the amateur feeling, in the finer sense, was preserved, and has marked the history of the Guild ever since.

The first offering of the Guild, Benavente's *The Bonds of Interest*, was a *succès d'estime*, a failure financially, and hardly more than a respectable try at something fine in the opinion of press and public. But with the second production the organization leaped into fame and sufficient wealth to project a new season of five plays. In their presentation of *John Ferguson* the group achieved one of the most satisfying productions of their entire history. Their play record in the six seasons since has been rich in novelties, spotted with such large successes as *Jane Clegg*, *Heartbreak House*, *Liliom* and *St. Joan*, and with such fine controversial but stimulating things as *From Morn to Midnight* and *Processional*. There have been mere fillers too: plays patently not worth the time and expense spent on them, and others that failed to register in the acting and staging. Occasionally virtuosity in the acting, together with the Guild reputation, has saved a not important play—such as the current *Guardsman*. Or did the Guild eye to sex interest—which has worked more than one would expect in an art theater—have something to do with it?

Speaking of staging that failed to register, let me hasten to add that I do not mean merely the visual effects of setting and lighting. In these departments the Guild's presentations have been almost uniformly satisfying. No other achievement of the group has been so creditable at all times as its series of stage investitures; and no other organization has turned up a scenic artist with quite the same unfailing craftsmanship and sense of appropriate decoration that Lee Simonson has shown. In the field of the new stagecraft the Theater Guild has set a sustained standard worthy of any art theater.

In the matter of acting, the story runs quite otherwise. *John Ferguson*, *Jane Clegg*, *Heartbreak House*, *Processional*, these remain in mind as about as well acted as one could ask—and the first two will go down in history as models of ensemble realistic playing. But only too often there are "holes" in the Guild casts. In the three current plays, two of them beautifully acted in the main parts, there are flagrantly bad bits that seem to me to spoil the ensemble effect. And occasionally a very fine play has been all but ruined in the playing. It is not that the Guild has not had good actors. Practically all the experienced players one would want to call to a resident repertory company have appeared on the Guild stage at some time during the seven seasons. It is rather that the direction has been uneven. The organization has failed to find a really great director, and sometimes even an adequate director. Trying out half a dozen American and imported artists in this work, and occasionally falling back upon a member of its own inner group, it has yet to put down among its permanent officers the name of a producing director. Its future success as an art organization perhaps depends chiefly upon the solution of this directing-acting problem.

In form of organization the Guild is practically a privately owned institution, in the hands of six individuals. But by virtue of the unselfishness and taste of the owners, and the coöperative interest of a large subscription audience, it takes its place among institutions serving the public primarily for the sake of service. As such it has enjoyed generous aid at two points in its career: at the start when Otto Kahn put a theater at its disposal, for better or worse; and when it was ready to build its new home, at which time its subscribers and friends bought its bonds on what is probably a very good investment plan, but without absolute certainty of the return of principal and interest. The owning Board originally showed its faith in the membership-audience plan, and has never swerved in its determination to become absolutely self-supporting and independent through this best of all forms of subsidy. It has been richly rewarded thereby: the subscribers increased in number from 135 in the first (short) season, to 500 at the beginning of the second, to 6000 at the beginning of the fifth, and to 14,000 at present. With 14,000 subscribers the Guild is independent, in the sense that the expense of any production that may be planned is covered by money in the bank before a seat is sold from the box office. Such independence means a greater responsibility on the owning group—artistically. With that independence and its monumental new building, the Theater Guild enters upon the second period of its career with the eyes of the progressive world upon it.

The new Guild Theater is worthy of study by builders everywhere. In completeness of plant and suitability to purpose it is not likely to be excelled in New York. Its stage is unusually large, forty-nine feet deep and seventy-seven long, and has adequate and flexible lighting and rigging equipment. The absence of a sky-dome or any satisfactory substitute is the only handicap to staging in the most approved modern fashion. There are typical organizational accommodations throughout the building: lounge, club rooms, library, offices, studios, school rooms, rehearsal hall, green room. In general plan, too, the architects seem to have used shrewdly and wisely every foot of the expensive New York real estate. Only one compromise is noticeable. In its decorative features, in surface design and furnishings, the building is frankly period stuff: a monument to the unoriginality of the American architect. It is spacious, comfortable looking, better in coloring and decorative scheme than most—but certainly in its atmosphere not suggestive of the Guild's courage and independence and forward-sightedness. A laconic sentence in the official announcement tells the whole story: "The furniture is genuinely antique or skillful reproduction." The one best thing that can be said about the Guild itself is that it is neither an antique transplanted to New York nor a reproduction of anything existing, but a *living* institution, born of a current need and creatively endeavoring to fill it.

VI

The other full-sized professional group working toward art theater standards in New York is the Actors' Theater. This organization is far younger than the Guild, less firmly established in the community, without a home of its own, and still very wobbly in policy. But in the one matter of having established a truly fine standard of production, of ensemble acting against thoroughly adequate scenic backgrounds, it has surpassed any other native institution. That is a mighty good first step toward a mature repertory art theater.

The Actors' Theater was established under the name "Equity Players" in 1922. It took its name from the Actors' Equity Association, because the Council of that larger organization appointed the first Board of Directors of the Players, and also because one hundred and fifty A. E. A. members financed the first season. After two years the name was changed to the Actors' Theater to avoid further confusion with the now unconnected parent organization.

The Equity Players immediately elected to give up the more radical experiments usual to organizational theaters, and leased a playhouse on Broadway, thus coming into direct competition with the commercial managers, and becoming dependent upon the casual floating public. A policy of presenting almost exclusively American plays was adopted, and in the first season eight of the ten regular offerings were native, one revival and seven new. In that alone there is a record—for I think that no professional producer with anything like the same standards ever produced so many in so few years—but it almost killed the organization. Among those plays were three at least that were exactly the sort of material that a serious progressive group should present: Jesse Lynch Williams' *Why Not?*, David Carb and Walter Prichard Eaton's *Queen Victoria*, and a courageous thrust into new and untried fields, John Howard Lawson's *Roger Bloomer*. The second season ended, too, with Rachel Crothers' *Expressing Willie*, somewhat less serious but dignified enough and a great financial success (which the others had not been).

By the beginning of the third (current) season, the directors were feeling the pinch of their all-American policy. They were obliged to face the fact that no one producing group can find every year five new American plays upon which it can conscientiously gamble an average of fifteen thousand dollars per production. After one American try in the new season, the directors turned tail and ran for the cover of Shaw and Ibsen. By putting into *Candida* and *The Wild Duck* the best of acting and directing, the organization scored successively two combined artistic-commercial successes, thus crystallizing in the minds of public and critics that here was a group actually committed to the ensemble ideal in acting, and offering examples of which any European art theater might be proud.

The Equity Players also announced plans for producing at special matinees plays that should be seen in New York but that seemed not to warrant regular evening runs. They thus produced Charles Rann Kennedy's *The Chastening* in the first season, and Ibsen's *Hedda Gabler* in the second, to appreciative audiences and with reasonable financial profit; thus demonstrating a further method of providing for New York playgoers the unusual and special things that otherwise never are available. If the Actors' Theater this season paid dearly for its matinee series, through an excess of ambition, it does not disprove the heartening proposition that this theater or the Guild or any other with an uptown house can almost double its service to the community by bringing in special matinee engagements. The secret here is to make the production just as fine as that of any play in the regular series, never skimping in casting or staging, but choosing plays that do not make large demands in the mounting.

In form of organization the Actors' Theater is a non-profit-making corporation, controlled by a board of thirty-five actors, with a paid administrative staff that makes all decisions except on matters of policy and play choice. Production is in charge of a Producing Director, although he does not stage all the offerings of the theater. Pledges to meet any losses sustained by the organization were signed during the first season by a large group of actors, and in later seasons by a wide group of interested and public-spirited businessmen. The theater has therefore been subsidized, in a piecemeal way, and could have drawn for losses up to one hundred thousand dollars in any season.

The mistakes made by the organization have been many, as they will naturally be in any effort to break new ground; but they have usually been in the nature of good experience. They need not be mentioned here except as they may prove illuminating to other groups starting the same path. Most hurtful of mistakes has been that of neglecting to build up permanent support in the form of a subscribing audience—and this season in not keeping faith with what membership audience it had. Each year has seen only a half-hearted attempt to bring in renewals and new members—because the controlling Board was not wholly sold to the idea of a subscription-supported theater. But nothing is truer than that the safest anchor to security for such a theater is in a membership audience, and that the members must be given as many plays as they are promised.

The organization's standing is such, on the basis of an established standard of production, that its mistakes are bound to be forgotten in the greater value of its service to a community that wants great plays beautifully acted. Its future is likely to lie in the double duty of providing old and modern classics adequately presented, and encouraging the most promising

American playwrights by occasional productions. A balanced repertory of this sort, with the emphasis on ensemble acting, is sure to find its public, granted even reasonable wisdom on the part of the organizers.

VII

The Community Playhouse groups at Pasadena and Santa Barbara have occupied beautiful new buildings of their own this season. Nothing could better indicate to the world the position they have assumed in the life of their respective cities than these extraordinarily fine homes that have been supplied for them. Both organizations have grown gradually from the most unpretentious amateur beginnings (although the Pasadena project had as forerunner a professional stock company that failed); and both went through the usual years of struggle and uncertainty. Now they have emerged as permanent foundations for the advancement of creative dramatic art.

These two are of a special type of art theater that is particularly suited to towns where there are few road company performances, and they lean to an occasional typically Broadway play along with their Shakespeare, Shaw and O'Neill. But they are living examples of the change that has come in a decade in communities of every sort and size: the change that brings recognition of the theater as a public service institution, as necessary to wholesome and rounded-out cultural life as libraries, schools and art galleries.

The Community Arts Players of Santa Barbara re-

The Pasadena Community Playhouse, recently built for one of the long-established little theater groups in California. (Elmer Grey, Architect.)

cently played a full two-weeks run of *The Beggar on Horseback*, breaking all records for either amateur or professional engagements in the town. Their theater has also gone far toward establishing itself as a community center in a much wider sense than as merely a dramatic producing concern. In this case the theater and the Players form one branch of a larger Community Arts Association, thus integrating into the wider pattern of the æsthetic expressiveness of the city. In Pasadena the Community Playhouse Association is a separate entity, organized only for dramatic activities. Its history over seven years, from struggle, debt and neglect to a position of security and recognized artistic service, with a plant of its own representing an immense expenditure in money,* energy and time, is an inspiriting record for organizers everywhere.

One other organization may serve as example of the crystallization of the little theater idea into the mature art theater consummation. At Cleveland the Playhouse group started nine years ago as an experimental insurgent organization. At first it was hardly more than a laboratory stage. Under Raymond O'Neil it developed slowly, almost obscurely, testing the possibilities of amateur acting in unusual plays, and seeking those special technical means suitable to unpretentious art theater production. On the firm foundation thus laid, a later director, Frederic McConnell, has built up an acting organization that serves its city adequately

* For the information of those who may be dreaming of the same sort of plant, let me add that the money value of the Pasadena Community Playhouse is nearly $400,000.

with the best plays of past and present. Here again the community is so appreciative that a site for a full-sized theater has been given and a building fund is well on the way toward completion. The new Playhouse will be equipped with two complete theaters, a larger one for the regular repertory offerings, and a small experimental annex.

VIII

My historical work is done. I have tried so far to show how the American theater came to its recent distressing position, and how a somewhat similar condition in Europe led to the establishment of art theaters as a natural corrective. I have sketched our own beginnings and our most important examples of progressive theaters. Now I wish to explore in more detail the changes which have already come and those which are implied in the art theater movement, trying to shadow forth ideals, describing methods of production, and outlining systems of organization. I hope that I may possibly arrive at conclusions which will help to stabilize the whole progressive movement, which will perhaps enable workers in the little theaters to arrive at a clearer conception of the ultimate idealistic goal, and which, finally, may inspire artists and playwrights with renewed determination and renewed desire to do creative work.

CHAPTER IV

IDEALS OF THE ART THEATER

When one is asked what warrant there is for setting aside certain theaters and applying the somewhat pretentious name "art theater" to them, one's widest justification is likely to be expressed in the word "idealism." No theater that is visualized as other than thoroughly idealistic will come to the estate of an American *Vieux Colombier* or a native counterpart of the Moscow Art Theater. Insofar as our "leading" progressive groups have departed from the idealistic point of view, they have measurably failed to fill that highest place that is vacant among the theaters of the land. Idealism in this sense may in itself be put down as the first ideal of the art theater.

We all compromise up to a certain point, and our individualistic idealism is thus a matter of degree. But somewhere along the line there is a division point between those who in the larger view can be called idealists, and those who are largely opportunists. I have been too much in the gambling game on Broadway not to have had experience of the temptation to compromise, to grasp the opportune thing. My weight has often fallen in that direction when the question came up in the organization I have recently been with. But I emerge from three seasons of service in competition with the business theater, if not of it, more convinced than ever that a high idealism is the finest gift that a worker can bring in the struggle that is before us. The one valid criticism that is hurled with any frequency at the prosperous Theater Guild is that the directors have compromised with public demand, that they have chosen their "advanced" plays with an eye not entirely to merit, but considerably to sensationalism and sophistication. Not alone the uncompromising idealists, the extreme non-conformists who might lead us only to isolation and a rarefied waste place by their demands, but the ordinary eighty or ninety-per-cent idealists, have felt this, I think. The Actors' Theater disavowed at the start any experimental ideal, explaining that when they took on lease a regular Broadway house, they gave up the "special" type of play that could not stand competition for Broadway audiences. But this organization too has compromised a little too frequently, in that it has let other plans wait as soon as a production showed profitable box office returns. A first axiom of the institutional theater is that it must have in mind always the ultimate thing, the keeping of faith with its subscribers, the permanent plan of productions, the enduring effect of its continuance or withdrawal of any particular play. Idealism, then, in play choice; and idealism in holding unflinchingly to the more difficult course when money-opportunism suggests an easier material way. This *general* idealism must come even before that devotion to a high standard of production which is the least difficult of the art theater aims to identify as distinctive.

I

There is, it seems to me, a distinguishing quality by which the typical art theater production can be marked off as different from the ordinary production in the commercial theater. Call it spiritual unity, rhythm, style—what you will—there is unmistakably a quality about it, an earmark of higher art upon it: a something that distinguishes a production of Craig or Reinhardt, of Browne or Hume or Robert Edmond Jones, from that which bears, let us say, a Shubert or Woods or Brady label. It is, at the moment, the difference between the beautifully *complete* Actors' Theater performance of *The Wild Duck* and the half dozen other offerings along the same street. The attainment of this quality, moreover, the development of artists who will expend their genius to bring this completeness to the stage, and the establishment of permanent companies to perpetuate it: this is perhaps the most important problem in the theater world today.

There is—possibly only theoretically—in every important drama a latent art value, as distinguished from dramatic value, or acting value, or spectacular value. I cannot come nearer to expressing the idea in words than by saying that this "over-value" is to be realized in the theater not alone by a synthesis of the clearly marked elements of staging—by perfect coördination of play, acting, setting and lighting—but also by the spiritual transformation of the whole through artistic-theatric vision. This implies the existence of a director who is artist enough to harmonize the provisional or incomplete arts of the playwright, the actor and the scene designer, and at the same time develop, by a creative method of production, an inner rhythm, a complete theatrical unity.

It is conceivable that a certain play might be presented in a commercial theater with the dramatic "punch" stronger, the acting more striking, the settings more decorative than in a presentation of the same play at an art theater, and that the latter production would still be the more interesting and more satisfying. For the art theater method would impart a unity, a harmony of elements and a stylistic impression which the other would wholly lack. The true art theater will, of course, have better acting and stronger plays than the commercial theaters; but the existence of a distinctive art theater manner of production explains why plays put on by amateur or mediocre professional actors, by such organizations as the Washington Square Players or the Chicago Little Theater, or by the Neighborhood Playhouse or the Provincetown Players, occasionally afford finer pleasure than that usually experienced in the best commercial playhouses. This fact explains why these groups year after year find their faithful subscription audiences renewing.

The first ideal of art theater production, then, is not merely simplified and suggestive settings, or ensemble acting, or poetic plays; it is the attainment of this elusive quality which makes for rounded-out, spiritually unified productions. I used to call it the synthetic ideal—a name I have come to dislike, but for which I know no adequate substitute.

As it concerns the dramatist the synthetic ideal means that the playwright either must be the director of his own productions, or must submit his written work to the creative processes of an artist-interpreter—just as in music the composer must leave his work to the interpretation of a violinist, or pianist, or orchestra-director. The artist-director, if he be not the playwright, must in turn be able to grasp the inner rhythm of the dramatist's work, conceive settings, lighting, acting, movement, costuming, etc., in harmony with that rhythm and at the same time stamp the complete result with his own individual genius.

As it concerns the actors, the scene-builders, the electricians and the other workers on the stage, it means that they must always be obedient to the will of the director, working sympathetically, "with answering minds," to create the one desired impression. It is true that the actor may enjoy a certain latitude of interpretation, but it must always be within such limitations that it will not disturb the ensemble as visualized by the director. This carries the implication, of course, that the director must know the capacities (not merely the types) of all his actors.

The synthetic ideal is big enough to embrace many creeds of playwriting and many types of play. It has room not only for the imaginative, the symbolic and the expressionistic but for the realistic and romantic. The synthetic method is applied most easily to plays with a clearly defined "atmosphere" about them—the plays, say, of Maeterlinck or Euripides or Dunsany; but it is possible to apply it also to Ibsen, to Hauptmann, to Masefield, to Shaw—although here perhaps the director has need of even greater vision.

The written play itself confines the producing artist within certain limits. But since the director's work is creative, since he reinforces the poet's conception by bringing to the staging an originality of his own, no two directors will arrive at exactly the same result; each will impart his own distinctive touch, or evoke a particular mood. Thus the entire result, the effect in recollection, always bears the stamp of the personality of the artist-director; it reflects his peculiar manner of producing the play as distinguished from the manner of any other producer, and it reveals the quality of his individual artistic vision. In the spiritual "over-tone" it bears the stamp of his genius, and in the technique of production it is instinct with his "style." There is, of course, a give and take between director and actors, a modification through company "team work."

If I have given the right impression of what I mean by synthetic ideal, the reader will know that it can never become merely the concern of an over-specialized group, or the pursuit of a single theory of production. If any number of our little theaters become art theaters—that is, start definitely and intelligently the search for the principles underlying art theater technique—we shall have as many types of synthetic production as there are artists in the movement.

II

This elusive ideal that we have been talking about seems to me to lie behind the indeterminate longing, theorizing, and actual work of practically all the important insurgents of both Europe and America, from Craig, Stanislavsky and Appia to Browne, Jones and Geddes.

It is what Adolphe Appia sought when he tried to create an "inner unity" for the Wagner music-dramas by binding the setting and action to the music through atmospheric lighting. Taking his pattern of moods from the music, he designed a series of lighting effects in perfect harmony with the emotional and spiritual sequence of the drama; he subordinated the settings through simplification and by throwing over them a veil of light or darkness, really substituting creative atmosphere for the usual painted or plastic scene; and he intensified the action by cunning manipulation of light and shade, playing groups of actors against masses of shadows and bursts of light, or half-revealing them in foggy grays. Appia's great contribution to the modern search for an art theater technique lies in what he taught later artists about the harmonizing value of lights on a "sceneless" stage.

The synthesis sought by Gordon Craig is one in which movement, in a large sense, has an important part, and in which scene, color, lights, voice and music have place. In order to achieve perfect unity of these various elements, he would have the artist-producer be if possible playwright, designer of settings, lighting and costumes, and composer of the music, as well as director. In case he cannot write his own drama he must experience a complete vision of the original poet's intention. Craig goes farther than any other leader in his insistence upon the absolute necessity of a man of vision in the director's position, and he would give that man the greatest breadth of original invention. He writes: "I let my scene grow out of not merely the play, but from broad sweeps of thought which the play has conjured up in me. . . . We are concerned with the heart of this thing, and with loving and understanding it. Therefore approach it from all sides, surround it, and do not let yourself be attracted away by the ideal of scene as an end in itself, of costume as an end in itself, or of stage management or any of these things, and never lose hold of your determination to win through to the secret—the secret which lies in the creation of another beauty, and then all will be well."

That is a poet's statement of the art theater's problem and its ideal: "the creation of another beauty" while "concerned with the heart of" the dramatist's play, "and with loving and understanding it." In solving the problem Gordon Craig came to many radical conclusions, regarding subordination of setting, repression of the personality of the actor, designed movement, and the value of color and light in creating atmosphere, which have since become commonplaces of the new movement. He arrived at other conclusions that have been slower of acceptance. Because the average actor was unable to sink his personality entirely in that of the character played, because he could not make himself clay in the director's hand, Gordon Craig at one time gave the impression that he was ready to discard the living actor for the puppet. A world fond of picturesque iconoclasms took this as the essential clew to Craig's theory of the theater, and he has been constrained ever since to reaffirm his belief in the actor *in his place*. When he was persuing a synthetic art of the theater based on decorative movement of figures, colors and lights, Craig similarly seemed ready to discard the spoken word, as an interruption of the mood. Each one of these radical ideas must be taken in connection with the man's entire program of testing and revaluation. In all his experiments, through all his changing theories, the chief end has been, I think, the creation of mood, the evoking of a single impression in place of the scattered appeals of the usual dramatic production; and at one time or another he has been ready to discard each individual element if it did not fit in.

Since this first ideal of the art theater, this creation of another beauty, is outwardly visible only in the setting, the lighting and the method of acting, it is easy for the shrewd opportunist to pick up the external features and achieve a sort of caricature of the true art theater production without grasping the heart of the thing. The difference between the old sort of production and the new seems to lie entirely in the manner of staging; and so the astute commercial manager picks up a few mannerisms, gives out that he is staging in the new method, and draws a crowd. We have, indeed, had too much new scenery and too much new manner, and far too little new vision, new creative form.

Even so eminent a director as Max Reinhardt cannot be entirely freed from the charge of mannerism: he has occasionally made the method obtrusively evident, to the loss of the original author's intended effort. There is no doubt that he has achieved a unifying system; but the unity sometimes seems something superimposed by Reinhardt, and not a synthesis growing out of the heart of the play. The way of his working, nevertheless, is the right one. The entire production filters through his imagination. The following extract from an article * by Hugo von Hofmannsthal on Reinhardt perhaps will explain much about both his failures and his successes:

"He is so full of vitality himself that he sees everything, however remote in time or space, only as a slice of life. He sees everything with his own immediate sight and not at all from the historical point of view. And he sees everything through the eyes of the theater. The foreign artist, the foreign civilization, the foreign era—such restrictions do not exist for him. Lady Diana Manners, Maria Carmi of Florence, or Rosamond Pinchot of New York—he sees only a beautiful woman, a body with the possibilities of gracious movement, a lovely face that may command a certain range of expression. These are the things he uses. . . . He took certain things from the Japanese theater and from the theater of antiquity; he owes much to the ceremonies and pageantry of the Catholic Church. Venice, that dream city, its architecture and history more theatrical than anything else in the world, has always

* "Reinhardt as an International Force," in *Max Reinhardt and his Theater,* edited by Oliver M. Sayler. New York, 1924.

fired his imagination. No national procession that he watches in a mountain village, no picture that he sees in a museum fails to enrich him, but what he makes of it all is something peculiar to himself, and something apparently inexhaustible."

III

"Stylization" in its broadest sense means the unifying of the play by carrying a definite "style" through all parts of the production. In this broad interpretation the term is a synonym for synthetic treatment. Stylization has recently been narrowed by many writers to mean the application of individual style to the play's settings. But even when the unifying process is thus confined to the *mise-en-scène*, it is still a powerful factor in imparting continuity and singleness of impression to the production.

It happens that the designing of appropriate settings is the direction in which all countries have made greatest piecemeal progress toward the new ideal. The artists concerned have developed certain inventions which are definite aids to the attainment of synthetic effect. New lighting systems make possible the creation of atmospheric effects which are delicately attuned to the most subtle emotional or spiritual values of the play; new mechanical devices make possible rapid change of scene, thus doing away with the long between-acts waits which used to do so much to destroy continuity of interest and mood; and adaptable settings, wherein certain elements remain through several changes of scene, carrying a subconscious sense of oneness through several scenes, bring a new harmony of background. William Butler Yeats writes enthusiastically of a lingering "tone" of restfulness and beauty running through a series of arrangements of Gordon Craig's screens. Lee Simonson has tied together several Theater Guild productions with the extraordinary visual continuity of his settings, and Robert Edmond Jones has often achieved a sustained outward beauty that added immeasurably to the impressiveness of the production.

It may be that through the search for the ideal, through applying the unifying principle to the best plays we now know, the art theaters will evolve new forms of drama more beautiful, more complete, than any so far developed. Perhaps that decorative, typically theatric, de-humanized art which many of us have visualized fleetingly while we dreamed over the pages of Gordon Craig's essays will become a reality when the art theater method is studied, played with, and carried to its most characteristic achievement. It may be that Claude Bragdon and Thomas Wilfred will bring new wonders out of the art of moving color; or that Maurice Browne, Cloyd Head, Robert Edmond Jones and Norman-Bel Geddes, already pioneers in America's pursuit of an art theater technique, will prove that beyond all the experiments with the story-plays of the playwrights there lies a sort of rhythmic art of the theater as yet ungrasped and only half-guessed. But until we restore æsthetic unity on the stage, until we fit the play again to the theater and learn thereby the secret of unified impression—until, in short, we follow up the first ideal of the art theater,

Scenes from *Malvaloca* as produced by the Actors' Theater. The settings, by Woodman Thompson, illustrate the use of a "unit" decorative scheme.

complete imaginative-theatric production, we cannot achieve what lies beyond.

IV

Approaching the art theater from another angle, it is easy to distinguish another ideal that has been sadly neglected by the commercial playhouse—a minor one, when measured beside that so far considered, but important. It is the experimental ideal. Recently a group of little theaters has come into existence devoted entirely to the trying out of the work of beginning playwrights and stage decorators. Such theaters seldom make any claim to the creation of finished works of art. In the first place they are usually crippled by inadequate stage equipment; in the second place they prefer to concern themselves with art in the making rather than with the polished product. There is a legitimate place at present for such theaters; they are, indeed, immensely important because they offer almost the only laboratory facilities for the playwright who refuses to play the game in the commercial way, and for ambitious young artist-directors.

These theaters seem to me to be a sort of between-times expedient. They are a first step toward the establishment of an adequate non-commercial theater. When the American art theaters are built on their foundations, the experimental ideal must by all means be preserved; but all the present crudities should disappear in the performances before a public. Perhaps I am over-sensitive in the matter, but I squirm in agony when the rough edges and the dull tools become apparent to an audience. I want the theater at the time of announced performances to be a gallery rather than a studio.

The point is that there must be a corrective to its tendency to become a museum; and adherence to the experimental ideal keeps open the flow of life-blood of to-day and crystallizes some of the illuminating vision of to-morrow. But few mature art theaters will care to subscribe to one of the mottoes of the Provincetown Players: "The difficult is our special task—or we have no reason for existing." Nor do they want to become experimental in the sense that Professor Baker's famous workshop theater, or the Carnegie Institute Theater, is experimental.

It is more likely that the art theater will have its workshop annex—hoping that the proximity to youthful thinkers and radical young artists will serve to keep it from hardening into preoccupation with the plays, theories and methods that were new when it was young but will inevitably be outgrown when it is old. Thus it will provide for the author who is not quite ready for a professional production, facilities for seeing his play acted on a stage; and he will learn more in that way in two hours than in ten years of studying and writing in his library. The Wisconsin Players and other little theater groups have their workshop stages, whereon members try out their plays before carrying them out to larger audiences. The Moscow Art Theater has its "studio" for the training of young actors and the try-out of young ideas. The Theater Guild has arranged quarters in its new building for a school, and already has its "junior" group of workers. It also has followed the system of giving each season two or more special performances for its subscribing members of a play considered too "advanced" for its larger public. The Cleveland Playhouse is planning two complete theaters for its new building: one of 600 capacity for its regular repertory productions, and one of 200 capacity for try-out or studio purposes.

As a corollary to these paragraphs on the experimental ideal, I might have added more on the ideal of experimenting and working *slowly.* In New York our rush is such that we seldom find time for that exceedingly valuable thing called *contemplation;* and I am afraid that most of the little theaters are fashioned in the image of New York. They all want to "get something on." The idea that a man or a group might write and think and experiment and rehearse a single play for a year is too fantastic to be considered by any group living in the present. And yet the finest new things will come that way. Nor is it even usual to rehearse a play until it is ready; a date is set, and ready or not, the curtain must go up that night. This ideal of slow, contemplative, craftsmanlike approach to the problem of production, is, I imagine, the last that will be grasped by our American go-getters in art. But a reminder of it should be pasted on the walls of every director's office in every progressive theater in the land.

In New York Richard Boleslavsky has established his "Laboratory Theater" for the sake of this slow and considered approach to the founding of an art theater. For two seasons he has worked with his students and acting company, without being ready to stage a performance for the public. He writes * feelingly and illuminatingly on the matter:

"To contemplate, to search, to create—for this there is no place. There are no laboratories of the theater, there are no tense experiments and achievements, no tedious labor discovering new forms, no fling of imagination, no joy of attainment. There is no creation, there is only repetition and occasional blind luck, only occasional, as in a card game.

"We hear a fateful tragedy in the words of Gordon Craig, denying the actor and the living Theater, Craig who is himself a living Theater;—in the words of Eleanore Duse who can 'no longer serve her God' in the modern Theater, Duse who is herself the Goddess of the Theater;—in Reinhardt's leaving the Theater he created and in Stanislavsky's dream of working far from the world of the theater with a small group. Why do all these great souls, burning with the flame of the holy spirit, leave the contemporary theater? The reason is very simple; it is because the contemporary theater has become a shop, a department store, in which ready-made and labeled goods are sold. But where those goods are created, where their qualities are verified,—nobody cares. As a matter of fact, there are not more than two or three places in the whole world where these points are regarded to-day. Yet a real artist cannot only sell his wares,—he must be free and must live in a congenial atmosphere, he must have his own creative laboratory,—and there are no such laboratories. . . .

"The creation of such laboratories of the theater requires the consecration of its members to the work of the theater with its disappointments and blunders, its truths and revelations. In such laboratories there is no place for people who wish to make a quick fortune. The groups must be very

* *Theater Arts Magazine*, July, 1923.

small. Some of the performances should not even be open to the public. During the first five or six years each laboratory would barely be able to maintain the fifteen or twenty people working in it. But any such laboratory could push forward the theatrical art of the country twenty years. It could become finally a successful repertory theater, ready in its turn to cede its place to new laboratories, young, fresh and as enthusiastically searching for newer forms."

V

An obvious but often neglected ideal which every art theater should keep before it is that of sound business management. When the little theater groups righteously and courageously revolted against the business monopoly of the regular theater, they scorned the good as well as the bad of the commercial system. In the regular theater the artist had been obscured in the businessman; now the businessman was lost in the visionary artist. The result has been a notorious series of financial failures among little theaters. The fault must be corrected as the change to the estate of art theater is made. To quote Winthrop Ames, it is necessary "to avoid the artistic disadvantages of purely commercial management, and still to remain self-supporting"—which is to say, self-supporting under the terms of whatever endowment the theater may have. Of this ideal I shall say more in the chapter on Organization and Management.

VI

Many little theaters have set up what they call an ideal of intimacy, by which they mean that they want to bring the audience into close *rapport* with the actors on the stage. The truth is that no production in the art theater is good until it does bring a sense of intimacy to the spectator. There are spectacular plays which may be fitted for immense stages and barn-like auditoriums but they depend on pageant-like effects, and are only episodically holding in a sheer dramatic way. Certainly any play which has to do with the art theater demands a representation which will hold the audience in spiritual communion with what transpires on the stage. It seems to me that this sort of play can be as intimately produced in a theater seating six or eight hundred people as in one seating one or two hundred. The ideal of intimacy is really included in what I have called the synthetic ideal; for if a mood is created, the sympathetic reaction will come as readily in the larger as in the smaller place.

The ideal of intimacy has even been destructive in certain little theaters. The crowding of stage and auditorium has destroyed the conventional relationship of artist and audience. The spectator is often so close to the stage that he is over-conscious of the actors as people. The spectators should be brought into touch with the action in such a way that they will find themselves moved, that their souls will be purged by their experience of the dramatic story; but it seems to me that a little perspective is useful here. Many of the devices adopted ostensibly to bring closer relationship are likely to do more harm than good. I am not even convinced that the apron stage offers any considerable advantages except in rare cases, and I think that the practice of bringing players to the stage through the auditorium is usually a "stunt" designed to attract by its novelty. We must distinguish more clearly between an art of the people—Percy MacKaye's "civic drama," in which masses of people participate—and an art presented by artists for the people to enjoy by seeing and hearing. The latter sort is likely to be more intimate than the other, and nothing is to be gained by bringing tag-ends of the performance before the curtain-line.

I find myself here on the edge of the subject of presentational or representational production—an intricate, argumentative matter which is outside the field of a book which is designed to be useful in practice and not at all concerned with theory.

VII

When one realizes all that the synthetic ideal implies, it becomes very clear that its attainment is impossible under conditions existing in most commercial theaters. Not only do the businessmen who monopolize the regular institution usually lack the necessary vision and artistic insight, but the great majority of business theaters are unequipped to solve the problems of art theater production, repertory presentation and subscribing audiences. The most enlightened of the commercial producers, Winthrop Ames, with his finely equipped and wholly charming Little Theater (too long leased to another), might by a mere change of policy take place in the pioneer ranks of art theater directors. But it is a transformation which seems to me possible to not more than three or four of those now engaged in the gambling game on Broadway.

What, then, will be the relation of the successful art theater to the business theater? So long as the art theaters were all crippled financially and the commercial theaters wealthy, the businessmen controlled "professional" production and all important box office receipts. They also took many of the best actors and decorators developed by the new movement, and they bought the rights to plays of the sort affected by the little theaters. Now that the New York situation has changed, however, to the extent that the "fine production" field is more in the hands of organizational theaters than in those of the avowedly commercial producers, it is difficult to predict what is the relationship ahead for the two forces. Already certain standards have been greatly bettered in all classes of production on Broadway. Most notably, stage settings are infinitely more satisfying than they were ten years ago. Acting is less slipshod. And there is no doubt that more fine plays are being presented in New York than ever before, which probably means that less trash is being produced—although in this particular season that cannot be construed to mean less sensationalism and less vulgarity.

No doubt the theater businessman will continue to take away a certain number of ideas, men and plays from the "outsiders," as they are proved to be of financial as well as artistic worth. But even though the businessmen can pay larger salaries—playing, as they do, to the "best-seller" trade—there will be advantages in association with repertory companies which the more sincerely ambitious actors, designers and directors will be quick to see. One of the phases of the struggle immediately ahead will be the competition for obviously able and versatile actors who are particularly fitted for service with permanent art theater companies. A commercial manager recently asked, somewhat jocularly but with considerable cause, how he could produce a certain play which he had been holding, when the Theater Guild and Actors' Theater were utilizing most of the important actors he specially wanted. It is a sort of competition that will grow in the next few years.

In the matter of securing plays, there is little sign of progress for the outsiders as yet. The financial rewards offered by the business theater are too enormous to be overlooked by the successful playwright in a world built largely on money-power. A few authors are willing to make sacrifices to give the Theater Guild or the Provincetown Players a script before it has gone the rounds of "the big offices." But the advantage is with the commercial producer—except in the case of the very young playwrights who are just budding into achievement. Some of them are imbued with just that same idealism which actuates the projectors of the art theaters. The thing that is needed, however, to put the insurgent producers on a par with the business producers in the play market, is for America to have a network of local art theaters covering every city of importance from coast to coast; * so that a play which proves its worth in Chicago can immediately be prepared for presentation by the artist-directors at the local theaters of Boston and San Francisco. There is already the basis for such an exchange, plays which are first tried out by the Provincetown Players, for instance, being seen later on the stages of a score of community and little theaters, and possibly in a hundred presentations within two seasons. Since the Provincetown group dug up *Fashion* for its successful stylized revival, it has blossomed in curious guises on stages all over the country (the spread of it being accelerated, no doubt, by the circumstance that no royalty payments were involved).

Nothing will be able to prevent New York from sending its endless stream of revues, musical comedies and plays of the moment's mode, with their "second" companies, to the road towns. But it is likely that on the road there will come a clear separation of the art theater from the amusement business; and the events that have to do with dramatic art will center at the native playhouse. For the present a typical art-theater production may occasionally go into the commercial circuit, but it will be the exception. This is true

* It is true that many American cities now have stock companies; but these are in no sense art theater groups. With almost negligible exceptions, they are organized to compete with the commercial traveling companies, and their standards in choice of play and staging fall to the business theater level. They feel that they must be in the high-rent district, and there is the consequent necessity of playing eight times each week and making weekly changes of bill—thus mercilessly overworking the actor and leaving ragged ends in staging. The average American stock theater is characterized by haste and compromise of art for profit.

not only on account of the artistic short-sightedness of managers in the majority theater, but because the art theater play by its very nature is unsuited to quick transportation, hasty installation and the interpretation of typical "second company" actors. The distinguishing mark—the sense of unity, the subtlety of mood, the attainment of the primary synthetic ideal—demands a theater and a drama of its own.

CHAPTER V

THE ARTIST-DIRECTOR

THE figure about which the activity of a successful art theater usually centers is that of the artist-director. He it is who gives the theater its individuality and its place in the art world. When one thinks of the Moscow Art Theater the name of Stanislavsky immediately comes to mind, the *Deutsches Theater* just as inevitably suggests Reinhardt, and for most people Copeau *is* the *Théâtre du Vieux Colombier*. Similarly several of our own nearest approaches to the art theater type have been directly associated with the names of directors: the Chicago Little Theater was clearly an outgrowth of the artistic vision of Maurice Browne, and the Arts and Crafts Theater was definitely stamped with the personality of Sam Hume. A considerable amount of the floundering, artistically, of the Actors' Theater, the Theater Guild and the Provincetown Players has been due to their failure to find immediately that sort of director. The whole ideal of the art theater, indeed, is such that it demands as the first step toward its attainment the training of a race of such artists of the theater.

I

The man who has led the fight for a new organization of the theater is Gordon Craig, and it was he who first insisted that the cure for present evils could come only with the development of a new type of theater artist, a creative, all-seeing, omnipotent director. In a frequently quoted passage which has become a classic among advanced thinkers in the theater he has indicated the need for artist-directors:

"I have many times written that there is only one way to obtain unity in the art of the theater. I suppose it is unnecessary to explain why unity should be there as in other great arts; I suppose it offends no one to admit that unless unity reigns 'chaos is come again.' . . . And now I wish to make clear by what process unity is lost.

"Let me make a list (an incomplete one, but it will serve) of the different workers in the theater. When I have made this list I will tell you how many are head-cooks and how they assist in the spoiling of the broth.

"First and foremost, there is the proprietor of the theater. Secondly, there is the business manager who rents the theater. Thirdly, there is the stage-director, sometimes three or four of these. There are also three or four business men. Then we come to the chief actor and the chief actress. Then we have the actor and the actress who are next to the chief; that is to say, who are ready to step into their places if required. Then there are from twenty to sixty other actors and actresses. Besides this, there is a gentleman who designs scenes. Another who designs costumes. A third who devotes his time to arranging lights. A fourth who attends to the machinery (generally the hardest worker in the theater). And then we have from twenty to a hundred under-workers, scene-painters, costume-makers, limelight manipulators, dressers, scene-shifters, under-machinists, extra ladies and gentlemen, cleaners, program sellers: and there we have the bunch.

"Now look carefully at this list. We see seven heads and two very influential members. Seven directors instead of one, and nine opinions instead of one.

"Now, then, it is impossible for a work of art ever to be produced where more than one brain is permitted to direct; and if works of art are not seen in the theater this one reason is a sufficient one, though there are plenty more.

"Do you wish to know why there are seven masters instead of one? It is because there is no one man in the theater who is a master in himself, that is to say, there is no man capable of inventing and rehearsing a play: capable of designing and superintending the construction of both scenery and costume: of writing any necessary music: of inventing such machinery as is needed and the lighting that is to be used.

"No manager of a theater has made these things his study; and it is a disgrace to the Western theater that this statement can be made."

In order to obtain unity, then, in order to stamp a theater production with the vision characteristic of all true works of art, Gordon Craig wants a director who is master at one and the same time of playwriting, directing the actors, costume and setting design, musical composition, and lighting. This super-artist would stage his production with no other helpers than skilled workmen.

I wish that I could have faith in the birth of a race of such artists; but I think that one such genius in a century is a generous estimate of the probable world output. If we are to go on to any sort of achievement in our generation or the next, it is probable that we shall have to violate Craig's principle to the extent of separating the functions of playwright, director of staging, and composer of the music. These three men may possibly work together in what may be called group-creation; but there probably is not in the world to-day one man combining in himself the talents necessary to discharge the triple creative duty satisfactorily. Nor does it seem to me entirely necessary that the artist-director should be able to write his own play and compose the incidental music. If he is able to visualize the play in its deeper, spiritual aspect—if he is able to find its secret heart, and love and understand it, if I may so paraphrase Craig's own words; if he is then able to do all the creative work involved in staging and rehearsing it; and if he finally is able so to inspire a composer with the feeling, the mood, of the intended production that the latter will invent incidental music in harmony with the other elements: then he comes as close to Craig's ideal as one can expect in a practical world. And that will be close enough to secure the salvation of the theater as an art.

II

While thus willing to accept a compromise version of Craig's ideal figure, I do not wish to get so far away from it as does that keen critic and stimulating writer, Huntly Carter. In his interesting book about Max Reinhardt [1914] he outlines a theory of coöperative production, under which the director is to be only a leader in a group of creative artists, including playwright, stage manager, designer of settings, and so on. I wish, nevertheless, to quote Carter's words at some length, if only to reinforce Craig's ideas about unity and direction as fundamental principles:

"Nowhere is the theater equipped or organized to give the widest expression to the drama of the soul. As it stands it is quite unable to serve as a house of vision. All that it can do is to show artistic intention, give hints, throw out suggestions, offer scraps of vision and imaginative interpretation, turn out pretty odds and ends of pictures, wonderfully pretty bits of imagination, wonderfully ugly bits of so-called realism, wonderfully deft bits of stagecraft. But nothing it has done or can do in its present condition has brought it or brings it within measurable distance of producing the complete vision, the design of the poet filled in by answering minds, unified and vital in all respects. . . .

"The demonstrable fact is that the theater always has been, and is still, a vastly inferior, imperfect, and disjointed instrument of dramatic expression. In England especially is this true. . . . And if the temple is imperfect, its priests, as Mr. Craig rightly maintains, are imperfect also. If the construction and mechanical contrivances of the theater are crude and bad, the human directing, controlling, and interpreting force is not much better. It lacks unity. In short, the great number of units engaged in the work of the production of a play are not properly organized as a body to give that play the widest and most complete expression. They have not a vision in common, but they interpret each in his own way. As a rule they are a spineless and disjointed crew, without the faintest conception of a possible unity. . . .

"The new and significant thing in the theater is the expression of the Will of the Theater by coördinated minds, each artist taking the keenest interest in promoting the artistic work of the theater, each artist desiring to attain the best effect, not only for his own sake, but also for that of his fellow artists. This is what may be called the expression of the Will of the Theater. It is individual and collective striving of the highest degree. Each artist wills to attain his best individual effect, yet wills to attain the same end as the other members of his group, an end which only collective volition can assure. Thus the Will of the Theater springs from a common action and a common sentiment, the love of the artist for the theater, and its function is to give the widest expression to the Will of the author. Thus Max Reinhardt interrogates the alternative which Mr. Craig puts forward. Apparently he has no sympathy with the Napoleonic tyranny, and aims to replace Mr. Craig's seven-headed director by a seven-headed group of sympathetic and efficient artists who will together produce something as great and individual as a Gothic Cathedral, with all its parts so powerfully and perfectly willed that its infinite worth is apparent to the least of men."

From experience I would say that the trouble with this sort of collective production is that artists—at least those who are original enough to count—find it difficult to work together harmoniously. Usually it is a case of one being strong enough to intimidate the rest, and thus able to "spread" his department at the expense of the others; or else the group breaks up in a row. Unless there is the utmost sympathy between the several artists, moreover, there is great danger that the old lack of coördination will creep in: the scene designer will conceive the play in one mood, the chief actor in another, and the stage manager in a third, and everybody's teeth will be set on edge when the opening night comes. Unless, of course, the director has impressed his individual conception indelibly on each associate at the very start.

Huntly Carter's ideas about collective production were clearly designed to fit Max Reinhardt's system. For Reinhardt is not a creative artist in Craig's sense; he is a very intelligent organizer who at least seems to leave many of the creative processes to others in the group of which he is leader. Each member of the group is supposed to be "a related part of the complete interpretative mind." But the student of Reinhardt's work soon discovers that he is by no means uniformly successful in harmonizing and relating the several elements. The fame of his productions rests more upon the even accomplishment of his excellent acting-machine, upon the pictorial splendor of some of the settings designed by "his artists," and upon certain outstanding productions, than it does upon the attainment of any such distinctive uniform and pervading excellence as that of Stanislavsky's company or in lesser measure of Copeau's. He has brought together the most remarkable group of assistant directors, scene-designers, actors and workmen ever associated in one man's theatrical enterprises; but it is not so clear that the collective creation of that group, under direction of an organizer rather than an artist creatively concerned with every department of production, has attained that distinctive "hold-together" quality which seemed, a few pages back, the mark of art theater production at its finest.

Lest, in trying to shade the meaning of the term "artist-director" as applied to Reinhardt, I have minimized too far his power of visualizing and coordinating a production, I wish to quote von Hofmannsthal's description of Reinhardt's method of utilizing the talents of his associates: ". . . He demands, as the foundation for his play, the creation of a great dramatist, or, at the least, of a notable writer who presents in an unusual manner some phase of modern life. And in order to give this creation its

Scenes from *Hamlet* as produced by Max Reinhardt at the *Deutsches Theater,* Berlin.

fullest dramatic expression (and nothing less than the fullest expression will satisfy him) he employs a host of individuals quite as a great painter uses on his palette a varied wealth of colors.

"He uses painter, musician, skilled mechanic, lighting expert, and ballet master—uses and squanders them in a manner totally different from that of any other theatrical director, glorifies them far beyond the limits of their own abilities—uses and squanders, in short, every person, every device, every talent, every idea, every nerve, every intelligence that appears above his horizon (and his horizon is broad) that seems capable of serving the theater or that can be pressed into the theater's service.

"He squanders all this material as unconcernedly as he squanders his own existence, so that his theater may live, a theater to meet the requirements of his vision—requirements that change every moment and always demand the utmost of brilliance, of harmony and intensity. For he is not the entrepreneur, not the founder, not the dramaturgist, not even the pioneer or forerunner; not avid of money or power, not concerned with ideas or system; he is the visionary—the visionary who seeks to realize his vision; and in its pursuit he displays extraordinary powers of organization."

III

Gordon Craig wants an artist-ruler who will not yield to his helpers any of the creative processes, and who will rule his workers as an autocrat; Huntly

Carter wants free expression in a group of artists, with merely an organizer to hold the group together. It is probable that the practical ideal lies between the two views.

The theater will accept Craig's figure in his general aspect of artist-ruler, but will free him from the necessity of writing his own play and music. This, it seems to me, is possible because: first, the playwright's work is in a sense a finished product, and there is no danger of a clash over it—his script is the starting point, and the director is free to take it or leave it; and second, music is so much an art of mood that the composer, once understanding the requirement, is extremely unlikely to produce a score out of keeping with the playwright's intention or the director's conception. These two points aside, I believe that Craig's described artist of the theater must and will be realized before there can be an art theater worthy of the name. He will combine the authority of the following "artists" of the existing theater: producing director, stage-director, designer of settings, designer of costumes, designer of lighting. For the work of these men is such that disarrangement in one direction means disarrangement in all the others.

He must *feel* the production in all its parts, and he must then have power to confirm or veto the contributions brought forward by those in the departments of lighting, acting and setting. But he does not necessarily have to do the work of all these men; indeed, he would be foolish not to simplify his own task by turning over to the helpers such tasks as their capabilities fit them to do. The distinction, perhaps, should be one based on *imagination*. His must be the imaginative conception of the effects to be created in each department. This leaves to actor and stage assistants freedom for self-expression within certain limits, but never to the extent of violating the quality or style of the whole as established by the director.

This middle view was recently summed up by Jacques Copeau as follows:

> "To achieve that harmony of effect that shall really impress at once the minds and senses of the spectators, there must be one man who, having first penetrated the secret, and, so to say, incorporated in himself the rhythm of the drama, having also assimilated the character of each personage in the play and the actions and reactions between the various actors, should be capable of circumscribing the outline of the drama, setting bounds to its extent, forming its contents, planning the decoration of the stage, lighting it, arranging its furniture, imagining the physical appearance and costume of the actors, regulating the physical evolutions of the scene, assigning to everything its place, to each individual his particular action; in rediscovering, in fine, in a world of make-believe, the natural movement and infinite variety of life. The producer is here the substitute of the dramatic poet." *

The theory concerning the artist-director has come to such general acceptance among thinking people that one very seldom hears argument against it except from those who, for business reasons, do not wish to see the theater led out of slavery. But occasionally a critic insists that the principle is wrong because it means in-

* *Theater Arts Magazine,* June, 1925.

jecting a second artist between playwright and public. The dramatist's work, the argument goes, should be put on the stage according to his instructions as put down in the stage directions, without change. That is exactly like saying that a musical composition should be played as it is printed and not by an artist; or, in other words, that a schoolgirl with reasonably good mechanical control can give a truer rendering of the composition than can a Paderewski or a Kreisler. A written play, when considered not as literature but in relation to the theater, is no more a completed work of art than is a music score. The processes of acting, rehearsing, and designing lighting and settings, are creative; and unless there is a coördinating mind, a binding artistic sense, the production will be as expressionless, as incoherent, as the schoolgirl's playing.

IV

The theater of the past has seldom if ever known the artist-director so completely as he is known in the art theater of to-day. What he brings may be modernity's real contribution to the stage. The growing complexity of means, with lighting equipment that can be made to bring much of new atmosphere and color to a production, and the constant enriching of the traditional background of the theater, add to the opportunity of the directing artist to evolve a full and sustained performance. In reading through the histories of the world theater, it is apparent that certain periods have been known as the golden ages of playwriting, of the strictly literary drama; others as ages of great acting; still others as times when spectacle and the "effects" of the stage machine reigned supreme. No one can speak with absolute certainty about early times; but one would like to believe that we are at the dawn of an age when the complete theater will be mastered as never before, when a greatly enriched medium will be utilized to its full creative worth. If periods out of the past have been willing to accept an incomplete art of the theater, for the sake of verbal poetry, or inspired acting, or beautiful or novel stage pictures, it is certain now that more people than ever before have been studying the entire structure and will resent being let down badly in any department. Direct, complete and intensified use of the entire means at the disposal of any art is at the very heart of modernism.

In fairly recent times, the trend toward complete expressiveness and coördination has been marked by the experiment and theorizing of some notable figures.

Goethe in his old age had at least a dim vision of a new art and of a new type of artist who would be its master; and Wagner had a very definite conception of a union of all the arts—but, be it noted, of a union rather than a synthesis. Then came Craig and Appia, outlining the new theory clearly and pointing to the methods of practical achievement. After them followed a few men who approximated the artist-director type—Stanislavsky, Fuchs, Starke, Reinhardt, Copeau, Linnebach, Jessner—and a host of more or less competent workers seeking the ideal, some rather successfully and others with half understanding.

Most of these men direct theaters in Germany. The German regisseur is, indeed, the world's closest approach to a living embodiment of Craig's super-artist. He seldom has more than a small fraction of Craig's own inventive ability, and he does not do his own playwriting. But he is usually an artist of taste, and his special work is the supervision of the production *as a whole;* he is charged not with creative work in one department, but with creation of harmony through his imaginative contribution to every department. He is a master of lighting, he designs the settings, he plots the production for the actors and supervises their movements and speaking.

But the German regisseur could not save the American theater to art, even if we could import him at pleasure. Our problems are different, and we must begin farther back, with a pioneer type of our own.

V

Of all those who can be listed among the artist-directors of America, the truest to type and perhaps the oldest in service is Maurice Browne. No one has more consistently refused to compromise over what he believed to be foundation principles of the art of the theater, and no one has been the center of more spirited controversies. And with it all he is practically unknown in professional theatrical circles.

Maurice Browne established the Chicago Little

Theater in 1912, and for five years he directed it through serene and troubled waters. The way had presumably been prepared to some extent in Chicago by the earlier projects of Donald Robertson and Victor Mapes, both progressive but by no means so special in appeal as the Little Theater. Browne adopted at once many of the principles already laid down by Gordon Craig, but practically unknown in this country. His theater was very cramped and his stage a mere box. His settings were simple to the absolute limit, his lighting as decorative as the small stage would allow, his choice of play more uncompromising than that of any other anti-realist of the modern groups. The plays Chicago could see at the tiny playhouse included those of Euripides, Synge, Yeats, Ibsen, Schnitzler, Wilde, Strindberg, Hankin, Dunsany, Shaw, Andreyeff, and less-known writers in the same field. The list is an index to Browne's tastes, and an indication of the tenacity with which he held to his faith that a theater should be impressed with the personality of its artist-director.

The things that should interest us here, perhaps, are Browne's background as artist of the theater, the effects of his theories on his own project, and his influence on the American struggle for a new theater. His training was not professional. He had a broad cultural background, was known as a poet, and had a passionate interest in all the arts. He was a typical outsider—and for thirteen years he has chosen to work outside the commercial playhouse. He worked with amateurs—although in a sense he made them professionals when he was able to begin paying meager salaries—and he trained them with the ideas of Craig, Dalcroze and Appia, rather than in the image of the existent American theater. His group during its five-year history was more concerned than any other in America with the pursuit of a suitable and distinctive art theater technique. Some of his productions failed badly—due more to inadequate acting than any other one cause—but others achieved a quality which Americans have seldom experienced elsewhere in their theaters. His choice of plays doubtless alienated his public—and one is constrained to inquire whether it pays even idealistically to disregard *all* preferences and prejudices except those of a very specialized inside group of workers, all under the influence of one director. Certainly it didn't pay materially, for the project ended in bankruptcy.

The question can hardly be answered except in the light of qualifications about the standard of production. On second thought, I really believe that the Chicago Little Theater list of plays, if produced in New York or Chicago or Boston to-day, with a real art theater excellence and quality in the performances—as well done, say, as the Moscow Art Theater does its Tchehoff—would "pay its way." If your performances are *not* so fine, then you can only trust your own conscience to tell you whether you are changing your play list to toady to your community or only to avoid attempting a play that your resources won't allow you to do well.

Browne went his uncompromising way, and

"failed," as they say, at the end of five years. But it is probable that the example of his sticking so long, without lowering his standard, did more than any other one thing, during the first decade of the movement, to encourage others to pitch their hopes high and to work away toward an ideal. And of course his methods of staging were a revelation and were widely copied, to the betterment of many a little theater group. As a writer he was able to spread his ideas effectively beyond the range his performances could reach. He wrote this as part of a plea for an art theater in America:

"The man or woman who would establish an art theater that is an art theater and not a pet rabbit fed by hand, must be able to design it, to ventilate it, to decorate it, to equip its stage, to light it (and to handle its lighting himself, or his electricians will not listen to him), to plan his costumes and scenery, ay, and at a shift to make them with his own hand; otherwise his costumer and scene-painter, if he be fool enough to have one, will do strange things to send him nightmares at dawn and terrify his wife; and in addition to all these things that are essential, he will, if he be a wise man, have the stage-conventions of the last generation at his finger-tips—not merely because some of them are useful and most of them deader than Lazarus and so avoidable with foresight and a good nose . . . but because he is establishing an art theater, that is to say, imposing a living convention on a dead one, so that it is as well for him to know what the dead one was, and why, for example, Pinero and Sudermann are of it, while von Hofmannsthal and Abercrombie are not. And finally he will know not merely the names of Nijinski and Craig and Fortuny and half a hundred more, but what they have done, and, most important of all, how and why they have done it. And the reason he must know these things, which the millionaire and the pauper dilettante who are dabbling to-day in the art of the American theater do not know, is that he is establishing an art theater which shall be the temple of a living art."

After the closing of the Chicago Little Theater, Browne spent several years with various theater projects on the Coast, made two brief visits to New York, and last season became director of the Theater of the Golden Bough at Carmel-by-the-Sea. It is there that he has been trying, with the ideal stage he so sorely lacked elsewhere, to harness his uncompromising vision to reality.

Sam Hume made history as an artist-director when he organized the Arts and Crafts Theater in Detroit and administered it for two seasons as a "successful" approximation to the art theater type. Experience on the commercial stage formed part of his background, but he had come into personal contact with Craig and had turned "outsider." He didn't believe as Craig and Browne did that a man should set up as an ideal absolutely the finest things he could find or vision, and strike for the attainment of those or nothing. He was canny and shrewd in his estimate of how far he could go with his audiences and not lose them. His principle was to keep in advance of his public but never take a chance of alienating it entirely.

On one point he and Browne agreed perfectly: The artist-director must be a craftsman in every department of production. His training as actor, designer and occasional writer had given him excellent background, and study of the regular and advanced theaters of Europe gave balance to his experimental work. The

Scene from Cloyd Head's *Grotesques* as produced at the Chicago Little Theater. One of the earliest and best examples of little theater stylization, as developed by Maurice Browne, director, and Raymond Jonson, designer.

breadth of his work at Detroit is illuminating as showing what problems the pioneer director of an American art theater is likely to meet. In the first place he worked with the architects of the Arts and Crafts building, and effected modifications of the stage plans which resulted in the creation of one of the best little theater stages in America. He designed the lighting equipment and supervised its installation; and he designed a permanent adaptable setting, including a modification of the plaster "sky-dome."

In the season's productions he was given full charge of every department of creative work, and while he enjoyed the coöperation of a group of artists, his word was final in every questioned detail. If he did not choose all the plays, it is at least certain that none was decided upon without his approval. He individually designed most of the settings, and he worked personally with the artists whose names appeared as designers of the others. He worked out every lighting effect. He tried out, and helped to develop by individual training, every actor. And he rehearsed every play, looking after all those matters of movement, gesture and coördination of action which, while not noticeable to the audience, are important aids to synthetic effect.

Nor did his services to the Arts and Crafts Theater end with complete responsibility behind the curtain. Much of the preliminary work of organization and management, which should be the concern of others in any mature art theater project, were necessarily left to him—as they probably will be in many another little theater where a professional director is called to a virgin field. He lectured extensively before schools, clubs and assemblies, and otherwise helped to interest the community in the theater. And he later arranged other lectures and a teachers' class in an effort to carry the results of the theater's work to a wider circle.

So far as breadth of duties was concerned, then, Hume proved himself the type of artist-director needed by the little theaters of America. At Detroit he staged a series of productions with standards of acting and setting which were as fine as any yet attained with amateur and semi-professional players, and considerably better than many productions by second-rate professional companies such as have been maintained at times by the Provincetown Players, the Washington Square Players and other groups competing with Broadway, or playing too steadily for amateurs to participate. It was while watching Hume train his actors for the Arts and Crafts Theater that I came to the belief that America has all the raw material for acting companies that will ever be needed, and that it is only inspiring directors and opportunities for training that are lacking.

It was in choice of plays that Hume compromised. He sandwiched the plays of limited appeal between thrillers and farce-comedies. He frankly wanted to please his audiences (and his backers), and he added a certain number of somewhat shallow plays with a wide and obvious appeal to those that were clearly in the art theater field. It is not for this commentator to say flatly that such an example of opportunism and compromise was reprehensible under the particular circumstances. It is clear, however, that the Arts and Crafts venture takes on less significance in the perspective of later history because there were too few really important plays concerned. Here, then, is the artist-director combined with executive and organizer, and finally compromising with his businessman-nature.

The example of Sam Hume has doubtless had great influence on the little theaters.* He provided a model of a sort of theater attainable in many communities where before there had been only social-dramatic clubs, and where a true specialized art theater might be considered ahead of its time. Hume's "adaptable setting" was copied on stages all over the country—a fine thing where there were artists to use it imaginatively, but doubtless a dead and puzzling thing to many a group that could not capitalize its capabilities. Hume also has lectured extensively, taught in summer schools, and otherwise added his large bit to the impetus back of the struggle for better theaters. Since leaving Detroit he has been director of the Greek Theater at the University of California, where he did important producing work which was only distantly related to the type of theater with which we are here concerned; and he has also found time to direct producing projects in Berkeley and San Francisco.

There are others of these artist-directors who have preferred to work entirely outside the "regular" thea-

* The Arts and Crafts Theater, under Sam Hume's guidance, also served the whole progressive theater well by sponsoring *Theater Arts Magazine* during its first critical year, helping to establish a permanent medium for the exchange of ideas.

ters—even scorning those of us who have become entangled in competition with Broadway, I think—and several have lifted their standards of acting and staging so far above the average little theater work that their organizations approach within measurable distance of the ideal art theater. Some of them will doubtless be called to newly organized professional art theaters, to work with what actors they like out of both regular and insurgent groups, and to carry on their search on ideally appointed stages. Among the best of these men in our provincial producing groups are Irving Pichel, long an assistant to Sam Hume and many times his first actor, but also a director of exceptional imagination and long training, and now making a notable success of the Playhouse at Berkeley; Raymond O'Neil, an uncompromising idealist and for many years director of the Cleveland Playhouse; and Frederic McConnell, who took up the directorship at Cleveland in 1921, after O'Neil's leaving, and has given the audiences there a notable series of typical art theater plays exceptionally well presented. I should at least mention also Nina Moise and Gilmor Brown, who have had such success at Santa Barbara and Pasadena—although I know their work less well.

Of the directors who have been identified chiefly with the professional, and usually the business theater, and yet have been considered closer to the new groups by virtue of their sympathies and ambitions, I am choosing two as outstanding: Augustin Duncan and Dudley Digges. To these should be added Robert Edmond Jones, although his background is neither that of actor nor that of director in the commercial theater.

Augustin Duncan is so much the type of commanding artist-director that he has not yet found his permanent place at the head of a theater—our businessmen-producers not being willing to turn over to anyone else so much of control as an artist-director should have, and a curious circumstance having kept him from a permanent producing connection with the two existing, thoroughly professional institutional theaters. As a matter of fact Duncan has acted as producing director for both the Theater Guild and the Actors' Theater, but in both cases at the very outset of their careers, when the organizers wanted to keep all important decisions in the province of a ruling committee. It is not a system conducive to the holding of a competent director. If he has a real vision of what he is after, he wants more of control than a group-directorate is willing to concede.

Duncan not only has been identified with these and other progressive projects here, but spent several years in Europe, where he came into close contact with Stanislavsky and other leaders of the new movement. As producer of plays of the type of *John Ferguson* and *S. S. Tenacity*, he is a master unequaled in the whole group of American directors. In these and half a dozen other important productions, he contributed a living emotional quality and a smoothness and distinction in performance that marked him as the foremost native artist in his field. Latterly Duncan has been directing an occasional play for business-producers, sometimes redeeming shallow plays by the quality of his staging, and sometimes happening on to something worthy of his creative work—*Hell Bent fer Heaven*, *The Potters*, *Kempy*, *The Detour*. But always one feels that these are incidents, that artistically he is marking time until he has the repertory company and the sustained opportunity he so richly deserves.

Dudley Digges, on the other hand, finds himself at the moment in the position of producing director of the Actors' Theater, and justly riding on the crest of a wave of popular acclaim, for his unusually fine productions of *Candida* and *The Wild Duck* (the latter directed in association with Clare Eames). Digges, like Duncan, has acted in a great many more important plays than he has directed; and he similarly has a background of association with many progressive projects. He originally came to America as an actor with the Irish Players, and since then he has appeared often on the stage of the Theater Guild. His most important contribution as a director before going to the Actors' Theater was in the production of *Heartbreak House* for the Guild in 1920. In *The Wild Duck* production he proved that he belongs in the list of the foremost half dozen directors in America, by virtue of the sheer quality of the presentation. Insofar as idealism goes, he is well qualified to act not only as stage director but as head of an organization like the Actors' Theater, and he fortunately came to the position at a time when the Executive Board of that organization had had enough of divided control and piecemeal direction. He is promised a resident company and a repertory system of presentation next season—a step forward which will keep the eyes of the progressive theater world focused on him.

If Digges and Duncan have been essentially of the "regular" theater, but feeling a constant drag toward "special" production and repertory schemes, Robert Edmond Jones has remained essentially the outsider who was pulled into the business playhouse as designer for many productions—but always seemed identified with the insurgent groups. For eight years he was known as artist-extraordinary to Arthur Hopkins, and only once or twice during that time did he timidly essay direction. Two years ago, however, in accordance with his own conviction that the artist-director should be designer as well, he turned to the larger work. Since that time he has been one of the directors of the Provincetown Players. In his productions for this group there has been evident a tendency to stylize the staging and performance in accordance with a naïve imagination, with a desire to preserve a freshness and simplicity sometimes discernible in the best non-professional acting and mounting. The result has not always been happy, with the sort of professional company the Provincetown Playhouse is able to hold together. But the productions have invariably been interesting as experiments, reachings after something as yet unattained on our stages; and the mountings have been immensely intriguing. In the general service of doing interesting things too difficult for anyone else in New York to attempt, in occasional stylistic stunts like the revival of *Fashion*, and in the very fine of *Hedda Gabler* that he directed for the Ac- 'heater, Jones has given indication enough that ikely to take, in the field of the artist-director, that commanding position he has so long held among American stage-designers.

Having thus written of Duncan, Digges and Jones, I want to skip over the names of others who may become regisseurs of our future art theaters—Frank Reicher, Edward Goodman, Robert Milton, Philip Moeller, Henry Stillman—because none of these has achieved quite the same important stature, balanced by vision and idealism; and because after all it is the types and not individuals that are of interest here.

I must say something, however, about certain of the *little* theater directors, the typical skippers of those frail and sturdy barks that sail on altogether amateur waters. I know many of them, and I sometimes wonder why they stick to their ships in the face of so many difficulties and discouragements. But then again I realize that just there is the most heartening fact about the whole insurgent movement. They stick because the country is alive with the urge to expression, the urge to find beauty through the theater. Money is usually scarce, quarters cramped, "talent" sadly in need of fundamental training—and to cap it, the elders are too easily shocked by any excursion into liberal drama. But four or five hundred of them are operating out through the country to-day. Some groups are guided by ex-professionals, some by recent college graduates, some by artists and writers with a flair for staging; and some have thoroughly competent, even inspiring direction from graduates of Professor Baker's course at Harvard or Thomas Wood Stevens' course at Carnegie.

Of all the little theater directors, those seem to me to be doing the finest work who are trying to keep their organizations simply and frankly what they are, community affairs, striving to attain as much of sheer dramatic value as they can, without an eye to imitation of or competition with the virtues or vices of the big theater. Frederick Koch, once of the Dakota Playmakers and more recently of the Carolina Playmakers, has been able to win over a whole state to a desire for drama in a few short years, so that dozens of towns look forward to the coming of his troupe as one of the red-letter events of the year. He accomplished it by forgetting that the business theater existed, digging up native actors, stimulating native playwrights to dramatize familiar materials, and then going out and offering his resultant productions wherever there were enough people living to make an audience. Seven years ago it would have seemed an outlandish idea for any hamlet in North Carolina to write to the State University asking that an acting company be sent to present plays before a local audience. But last year the University received so many more requests for visits of the Carolina Playmakers than there were dates on the season's calendar, that a second troupe is contemplated for the near future, a permanent State Repertory Company. Professor Koch writes: "The itinerary of the first State Tour, five years ago, included only seven of the larger towns.

In the season just closed [1923–24] we have played to approximately twenty-five thousand people in twenty-six North Carolina towns and cities—in the mountain country, in the Piedmont section, in the tide-water region." And their repertory is entirely home-made plays. Such is the miracle wrought by one director's imagination, independence and hard work.

Some little theater directors stress one phase of their work, some another—and arrive equally at success if they are sincerely interested in what they are doing, for its own sake and not as an imitation of Broadway or the Theater Guild or Maurice Browne. At Pasadena, Gilmor Brown has directed the Pasadena Comunity Playhouse for eight years, and during all that time has stressed the idea of community participation. I find a record which says that "no less than 5000 persons have taken part in the Pasadena Community Playhouse since it started." That includes committees of several sorts as well as players—but it is evidence of the successful attainment of an aim. So successful, indeed, that Pasadena has just built one of the finest (not showiest) playhouses in America for its Community Theater. So much again an independent little theater director can do.

CHAPTER VI

THE QUESTION OF ACTING AND ACTORS

When one surveys the whole field of the American theater, commercial and progressive, one soon discovers that, next to the problem of artist-directors, the most puzzling question facing the art-theater group is that of acting and actors. In the departments of playwriting and stagecraft we have at least arrived at a basis of intelligent experimentation, if not at some sort of substantial achievement; but in the matter of acting and actor-organization we are merely in a muddle.

In trying to arrive at some conclusions about acting and actors in relation to the art theater, I shall avoid those deeper questions of theory that fill most of the books on the subject. The presentational method as against the representational, the depth to which the player should emotionally feel his part, the need for imagination, inspiration and passion—these interesting matters I willingly pass by. I am not writing technically or theoretically for any particular group of workers in the theater. I merely want to inquire what are those simpler qualities in acting, from the spectator's point of view, which seem to have been lost from most of the exhibitions in the "regular" theaters during the last quarter-century. Are they qualities which should be lasting ideals of acting as an art? Are there any distinctive differences marking off the practice of that art under the synthetic ideal of theater production? It may be pertinent to inquire, moreover, what are the sources from which actors for the art theaters will come.

In the commercial theater the ideals of acting were pretty much obscured during the last twenty-five years. Insofar as they were chiefly those which concerned the development (and consequent personal glorification) of the individual actor, not such as would primarily contribute to the ensemble effect required in progressive theaters, they persisted. In the average little theater, on the other hand, the acting has merely "happened"; and if the insurgent groups have developed an ideal, it has been only that of unconvention—a negatively decent but somewhat barren ideal, which overlooks beauty of speech, distinction of manner and designed group movement. And in those few cases in which amateur and professional have joined hands, lack of inspired direction has left the companies on a low professional plane: they have exhibited neither the smoothness of action of the first-rate professional company, nor the freshness, the felicitous speech and the team-work which alone can make the amateur superior to the commercial player. That the amateur can at times be superior, no one who has had wide acquaintance with the little theaters can doubt. But in both little and big theaters, the acting has left a very great deal to be desired, with only a spotty sort of progress apparent in the last ten years.

I

Of the attributes of great acting which have been all but lost to the theater in the last quarter-century, the most sadly neglected is beauty of speech. In this country the average actor forgot quite amazingly that there is a legitimate appeal to the ear in words musically spoken, and our stage fell to a dead level of prosaic and slovenly speech. In voice quality and enunciation the standard set in any but our very best theaters was not appreciably superior to that heard in our barber shops or college halls—which is to say that it approached an ungodly combination of stridency and mumbling.

It is clear how the theater came to such a degraded standard of speaking. Some decades ago, as an aftermath of the romantic revival, perhaps, the art of acting became a sad caricature of its once beautiful self, through over-accentuation and an absurd artificiality. Quiet and restrained impersonation was lost in an excess of ranting speech and heroic attitudes. People accepted the exaggeration as art, and went to the theater to wonder seriously at the thunderation and windmilling. When the naturalistic movement swept the theater, the artificiality was destroyed, but nothing was invented to take the place of what had once been a legitimate added beauty of the theater production. Poetry of speech was allowed, so to speak, to pass down and out entirely. The actor jumped from an exaggerated conventionalization to a method which was supposed to be "perfectly natural." But one cannot capture the illusion of the natural by unrelieved, unconventionalized imitation of chance aspects of life—whether in speech or movement or form and color. Insofar as the actor imitates without betterment the language of the street and the shop, he loses the only thing that can make speech tolerable, not to say lovely, in the theater.

The first requirement for bringing beauty of speech to the stage is a purely mechanical one: clean enunciation. As a nation we are notorious for our slurring methods of utterance. We do not break our words and phrases cleanly. But that is not a reason for accepting careless speaking in a work of art on the stage. Actors should rather set an example to the nation. In an art theater, or in one that makes pretension even to near-art standards, this should be a first test of the actor's fitness. Walter Prichard Eaton recently put it up to the little theaters neatly when he wrote: "The rankest amateur ought to be able to pronounce correctly, and enunciate all the syllables of a polysyllabic word without swallowing the penult. If he cannot, he should be politely invited to become a professional and join Mr. Cohan's company. When you enter a little theater you ought at least to be confident of hearing better speech than in any Broadway production."

The second requirement is partly a matter of physical endowment and partly a matter of training: a musical voice and flexible register. There may be people with "impossible" voices. If so, they should stay off the stage; they are no more fitted to become actors than a one-handed man is fitted to become a pianist. But most voices, if not naturally musical, can be trained so that they are at least passively pleasing; and most of us possess undeveloped tone-registers of which we never even dream. It is the business of schools of acting and studio theaters to develop this quality.

But after all, the potentially musical voice is of small importance if it goes not in company with the third requirement: a feeling for the expressiveness of speech. For otherwise the golden instrument in the throat will die with its harmonies unawakened. A merely mechanical musical voice may, indeed, drive a listener to distraction: an actor may catch the physical trick of voice modulation as it seems to be practiced by such a distinguished actor as Edith Wynne Matthison, and prove to be merely affected or annoying, because Miss Matthison's sensitive feeling and an added enrichment out of her personal emotion are lacking.

This matter of feeling is a variable quantity and an elusive quality; but we may be sure that it is never absent from the true actor's endowment. It enables the herald to speak his one line in a manner worthy of his courtly surroundings; and it enabled Sarah Bernhardt to ring every change of feeling through the music of her inflection. It is first of all a feeling for the rhythms of speech, for the cadences of the poet's lines; but more than that, it is a reflection and a suggestion of the subtleties and intensities of the emotions that lie hidden behind the action. For words are at best but symbols, and the impression called up depends upon the way of speaking. An inexpressive voice affords but a hard dry shell of meaning, whereas the same words from the lips of a master of speech may call up visions of passion or of calmness, of tenderness or love or sorrow—may afford overtones of feeling otherwise never captured.

These two things, then, we may assuredly demand of acting: that in the speaking there shall be a sequence of musical notes, a pattern of sound that will bring a physical delight to the ear; and that the voice modulation shall reflect a delicate understanding of the emotion and thought underlying the surface play of words.

Poetry of speech is not properly a requirement of poetic productions alone, but should pertain to realistic drama as well. For its beauty is not such that it detracts from interest in the action, but rather is an added loveliness. It is not ornament superimposed, and covering the structural lines, but rather a part necessary to the fullest expression of truth. There are, of course, poetic dramas which lend themselves particularly to musical interpretation, which allow the actor greater latitude in delicate musical intonation. There are even plays which, on account of lack of action, may be termed literary rather than dramatic, and which may still be staged satisfyingly through the appeal of the spoken poetry, for the sake of the sensuous beauty afforded to the ear. Such are several of the plays of Yeats and Dunsany and Maeterlinck. But even the realistic play can legitimately add the appeal of distinguished speaking. Unbeautiful speech, indeed, has no right place on the stage even of a realistic theater. An exhibition of commonplaceness there is no more to be pardoned than are those so-called naturalistic plays which reveal a photographic segment of sordid life.

II

After the music of speech there is a corresponding requirement of rhythm in the actor's movements. The statement sounds very stale and obvious—but it is unfortunately very much in place here, whether the book is being written for professionals or for amateurs. Not only must the actor's gestures be quietly expressive, but there must be a certain grace of bodily action, and a measured fluidity or rhythm in changes from posture to posture. Just as in the use of the voice, there must be overtones of feeling: the face, the hands, the body and limbs must interpret the subtler emotions which are not expressed in the larger action. For the face when used as a mask, and the body when directed as an instrument of rhythmic expression, can register shades of feeling which are impossible to even the perfectly modulated voice.

In the American theater there used to be generations of actors who possessed the subtlest powers of expression and distinguished grace of bearing. The older generation in the theater to-day has a charm of manner, a dignity of presence, which shames the average younger player. If this sometimes amounts to a romantic affectation or artificiality, so that we are apt to say disparagingly, "He has the manner of an old actor," it still is no argument for throwing away the principle. One has only to choose ten young actors and place them beside a typical representative of the old school, to know that we have lost a real charm from the making of our players of to-day.

The contemporary stage is peopled largely by personalities, each trained to parade individual idiosyncrasies or to rely on perfect "naturalness" of movement. For this the little theater players substitute no training at all. At least they have not spent those years of apprenticeship to experience which are necessary to perfect stage presence. One sometimes wonders whether one-fourth—nay, one-tenth—of the actors blithely appearing on little theater stages know that there is such a thing as scientific foot-work, or that the best of the older generation went through years of bodily training to gain ease of movement.

Expression on the stage may be partly a matter of natural feeling and intuition, although intellectual understanding and tortuous training have distinct place there too. But grace of bearing, the poetry of movement, can be developed in anyone with even an elementary sense of rhythm. Three of the leading art theaters of Europe, the Moscow Art Theater, the *Deutsches Theater* at Berlin, and the *Théâtre du Vieux Colombier*, in order to train their actors and students in the art of movement, have established courses in the Dalcroze system of rhythmical dancing. This, it is to be noted, is not in order to develop dancers, but to give players poise and action-control. Regarding the ideas of Jaques-Dalcroze, Huntly Carter has written as follows:

"The inventor has discovered that we all have musical rhythm in us answering to that of the universe, but very few are trained to express it. So he has provided a simple key which anyone can apply. He gives his pupils a quantity of musical notes, and leaves each pupil free to compose his or her own musical movements. In this view, every movement we make should and could be equivalent to a note of music, and, given the right note, there will be an harmonious response. If we are trained to realize these notes with the aid of music, soon we come to realize them automatically without its aid. Thus we may, if we like, learn to move through life in compositions in which spontaneous melody and rhythm, and not mechanical, logical, or meaningless actions, are the essentials."

It is perhaps too much to ask that any great number of Americans shall soon "learn to move through life" with anything approaching "spontaneous melody and rhythm." But we have the right at least to ask that our dramatic schools and studios shall train actors in the principles of some such system as that of Jaques-Dalcroze.

Beyond the matter of individual action, there is a wider group action, a designed relationship between player and player, which is too seldom practiced intelligently in the American theater. This is due largely to the lack of directors with sufficient artistic knowledge to make the play a concert of movement. The group-playing of the Irish Players comes to mind as an excellent example of unpretentious but intelligent related acting. Without emphasizing personalities, they always managed to throw the speaker into relief, the other actors falling into a background necessary to the picture but never interrupting the main motive; and there was about their stage groupings a gratifying smoothness, almost a fluidity of movement. In certain poetic productions, and particularly in those which rely upon the appeal to the eye as much as the appeal to the ear, it is possible to keep the grouping almost constantly in the realm of pictorial design. Maurice Browne is a genius in the application of the principles of pictorial composition to stage arrangement, and in several of his productions the figures have been so disposed that the eye was enchanted by a continual series of charmingly composed pictures. Such grouping can be overdone, to the harm of the spiritual content of the drama, with too obvious individual posturing or holding of group pictures—but so far it has been radically underdone on the American stage.

III

I do not believe that the quality of acting in the art theater will be different from the quality of acting in the finest productions of Winthrop Ames, Arthur Hopkins or Guthrie McClintic. But in the institutional playhouse everything will be directed first for the attainment of the ensemble effect. Beyond that it is difficult to point out any tangible way in which the acting at a typical art theater may be expected to differ from that at any commercial theater which may also raise its standard to include musical speaking, expressive and pleasing action, and intelligent, cooperative group-playing.

And yet as I look back over the playing at the institutional theaters here and abroad, I am tempted to add that *quietness of tone* seems a special quality of such companies as those at the Moscow Art Theater, the *Deutsches Theater* and the Chicago Little Theater. It is the note of reticence, of reserve power, of contemplative interpretation. (I am somewhat confounded just here by recollection of the way in which the Volksbühne company shouted its way through *Masse-Mensch*, in one of the most magnificently theatrical and abandoned performances I have seen in recent years—but that was in a wildly expressionistic play.) Perhaps it is that the quieter method of acting brings truer balance to the whole production, gives wider scope for developing the synthesis of all forces. There are times, surely, when it gives added opportunity for full expressiveness of the dramatist's meaning. William Butler Yeats, who has been particularly concerned with methods which would do justice to poetry spoken on the stage, once wrote in praise of the acting of the Irish Players: "It was the first performance I had seen, since I understood these things, in which the actors kept still enough to give poetical writing its full effect upon the stage." From practically all the European theaters in which the art theater ideal has been sought, critics report that the acting has been marked by a combination of quietness and distinction. Which is, perhaps, merely another way of saying that under the synthetic ideal, just as the setting must be unobtrusive enough to avoid interference with the action, and the lighting modified to harmonize with the mood of the drama, so the acting must avoid the flamboyant and the noisy, in order that the soul of the play may shine through unobscured by virtuosity on the actor's part.

The star system will have no place in art theater organization. In any serious production it is necessary that a balance of parts be maintained, that the emphasis be put not on one figure, with fillers to complete the picture, but on the ensemble.

The implication of the star system is, moreover, that it is the acting, and not the play as produced, that counts most. At least the system has so worked out in America, where the commercial exploitation of stars has had its most deplorable effects on playwriting. But a somewhat paradoxical result is noticeable: while the system began by exalting the art of acting at the expense of the other arts of the theater, it ended by all but destroying that art with the others. The big fellows among the actors, through being raised above the other artists of the playhouse, lost their perspective and failed to preserve the true relationship between the contributive arts, and so failed to grow bigger. And the little fellows tried to imitate the big fellows, and so fell into a mess of trickery, instead of developing their own native talents on a firm foundation. The temptation to create stars, moreover, was so great that certain managers began to push up

Examples of simplification of "scenery," approaching elimination, as practised in German art theaters. Above, a setting for *Der gerettete Alcibiades* at the Munich State Theater, and below, a setting for *Marquis von Keith* at the Berlin State Theater, both by Emil Pirchan. One of the chief gains to be noted here is the concentration of attention on the actors.

actors who, through prettiness or some other personal charm, were likely to catch the public eye, but who were lacking in the thorough training and depth of feeling necessary to make them truly great. A false standard was thus created, which has resulted in personality becoming the curse of modern acting.

It is true that the actor lends additional color to his rôle through personal distinction, through beauty, or strength or grace of manner. But it is nevertheless true that he must subordinate his own individuality to that of the character played. More than that, he must in the art theater freely submit to direction. This submission to authority does not mean surrender of the player's interpretative function; it means only that he must be concerned with the interpretation of the play first, and with his individual work after that. He may be just as great an artist under the director's guidance; indeed, he is likely to appear greater because he will be in perfect harmony with his surroundings. He is usually as free to interpret creatively as he is under the go-as-you-please system now in vogue in the American theater. He merely promises that he will keep his work within such limits that it will not upset the other elements of the production or clash with the work of the other actors. And these limits are set by an artist instead of a businessman or a businessman's stage-director. The scope for individual technique is as great as before, but within the limits of harmony with his fellows.

IV

What are the sources for actors to make up our mature art theater companies? In European countries the rank and file of the acting profession undeniably have had more of intensive and versatile training than their American fellows; and in general their cultural background is richer and their interest in all the arts broader. In Germany or Russia it might be only a matter of months to bring together a rounded-out, sympathetic and capable company for repertory production. Here, considering not only ability and willingness to work for the ensemble idea, but also the entanglements of commercial contracts and inflated salaries (due to the necessity for the actor to gamble a failure or two against every success), it would probably be a matter of years to get such a company assembled and settled down to smooth performance of a wide variety of plays.

Although in England the actor-manager system of production has had the same effect as the business-manager system in America, insofar as it interfered with development of companies devoted to the ideal of ensemble acting, nevertheless the standard of speech among English players is gratefully high. Ten years ago it was measurably higher than on the American stage; and if some of us had been taxed with the problem of gathering a permanent company for an art theater at that time we would probably have drawn very largely on English-trained actors, rather than struggle with the problem of how to pay the salaries of a hand-picked group out of the top crust of American players. Winthrop Ames, it will be remembered, long followed the system of importing many of his actors from London, and his companies achieved a distinction of voice and bearing that set a standard. He did not, of course, endear himself to the hundred-percenters who resent foreign invasion of any sort—and there are more cogent reasons than that why the organizers of our art theaters to-day should consider the native field first.

Chief of these is that America has developed an extraordinary group of promising young actors within the decade. This new generation is not always thoroughly trained in the fundamentals—is learning as it goes—nor has it had the advantage of versatile experience (the long-run system has killed that). But collectively it is intelligent, eager, receptive, and gifted with beauty and a certain expressiveness. Among the young women of ten years ago what group had we to match this representative list of to-day: Clare Eames, Katharine Cornell, Phyllis Povah, Florence Eldridge, Pauline Lord, Eva LeGallienne, Estelle Winwood, Winifred Lenihan, Helen Hayes, Ina Claire, Lynn Fontanne, Blanche Yurka, Margalo Gillmore, Jeanne Eagels, Mary Morris, Helen Freeman, Martha Bryan-Allen, Margaret Lawrence, Elizabeth Risdon, Lotus Robb and Helen Gahagan? These people are not all American-born, to be sure; but the great majority are, and all have long since become integral to our stage. There is talent there a-plenty for half a dozen art theaters. And furthermore you will find that most of these younger actors are sympathetic to the organizational ideal, anxious to break away from the long-run and the gambler's chance, to the permanency and wider artistic opportunity of repertory.

A critic recently remarked that given the players whom he had cast for the Actors' Theater productions of *Candida* and *The Wild Duck*, Dudley Digges could build a permanent company that in two years would rival the Moscow Art Theater company for fluidity and beauty of performance. Perhaps not quite so soon—but the material would be there. And so long ago as 1919 the Theater Guild gathered in its *John Ferguson* company a group of players that showed every sign of developing into an extraordinary acting machine—but a group that unfortunately was not held together.

I happen to know, however, just what was the combined salary roll for the *Candida* and *Wild Duck* companies, and I am sure that no economically run art theater could stand the pace—even allowing for reasonable concessions on account of year-round employment. Our professional art theaters will rather begin with groups including by no means so many well-known names, and develop their own younger players—as for instance the Provincetown group developed Mary Morris, and as the Neighborhood Playhouse trained Albert Carroll and Joanna Roos. The little theaters all over the country, too, are training (not systematically, but helpfully up to a certain point) countless young people with more or less stage aptitude. The best that can happen to most of these amateurs is that they reach the heights in their own little groups and stay there. But there is always that little minority that must be going on, temperamentally unfitted to remain in the small town, not satisfied with anything less than a try before the audiences of New York or Chicago. They will naturally drift to the institutional rather than the commercial theaters in those cities, having been nurtured on Shaw, Dunsany, Pirandello, O'Neill, Ervine, Yeats and other dramatists that smell less of business than of art.

From the profession as it stands, then, our American art theater companies will be recruited, *and* from the hosts that the little theaters are training. Considering that the permanent repertory company does not yet exist, we are rather embarrassed by riches—at least in the raw materials.

V

What of acting in the little theaters? We are not concerned with the groups that have never risen above the standards of the old aimless social-dramatic clubs. Nor can there be any advantage in exploring along that next stratum, that is amateur in membership and is saddled with an amateur or ex-professional director whose only idea is to effect a vague reflection of the tinsel glories of Broadway. But what of the acting in those hundreds of little theaters in the next group—amateurs in the better sense, intelligent, seeking expression, and as often as not directed by a graduate of the Carnegie courses, or by a fellow worker who has taste and imagination and perhaps a lot of sound experience. Whether these theaters are remote, undeveloped and not ambitious beyond a little stage, or in larger communities and advanced in ambition and experiment, they have this in common: they produce the same plays that are given by mature art theaters, and they somehow stage their productions with settings that seldom seem worse than the professional average—but their actors remain amateurs. They may have come to a point where they are carrying on a definite search for a distinctive art theater technique, and yet they cannot afford, even if they want, a paid company.

Should they want a paid company? If so, are recruits from the business theater a wise investment? Naturally, in the larger towns and cities, directors like Maurice Browne, Irving Pichel and Frederic McConnell want their little theaters to become economically sound art theaters—centers of dramatic art, as professionally administered as the public library or the art museum. It is a problem to be studied long in every individual case before casting the die. If the community is big enough and civilized enough, the need for the mature art theater is going to develop. Well, then, make sure that your project has been stabilized as a community affair, and then begin to professionalize *out of your own group*. That is, develop your own actors and scene designers and directors until, when the town demands more performances than amateurs can afford to give, they are worthy of pay. Make your own professionals as Maurice Browne made his at the Chicago Little Theater or as the Irish Players made theirs. But don't get in the sort of business-theater professionals you can afford.

For all the fine pioneering work done by the Washington Square Players, there was a weak link in their chain—in their acting. Putting together amateurs and professionals simply did not work. I often felt that their productions missed both the freshness of good amateur performances and the ease and finish of the best professional playing. Let me call into evidence the work and opinion of Sam Hume.

At the Arts and Crafts Theater he had only amateurs in his company, with results that compared favorably with the work of the Washington Square Players. Certainly the acting was no more ragged in general, and in the directions of speaking poetic lines musically and creating group-harmony it was superior. Hume's summary of the situation runs like this: At the present stage of the art theater movement we are limited, by the small audiences so far developed for the best forms of drama, and by certain exterior circumstances, to a small expenditure each year. If a little theater pays actors' salaries it cannot do justice to the other demands of progressive production. The class of actor it can afford to pay, moreover, is not able to do as good work as the best type of amateur. It is unwise to pay a few "leading" actors and then fill in with amateurs, because one thereby creates an undemocratic atmosphere and a basis for petty jealousies and disputes. It is better, therefore, to use only amateurs, at least until such time as the theater can afford the very best professionals.

Amateurs submit more willingly to direction; they have not the professional actor's obsession that the old method is right, and they conform to the ensemble method more easily. They are working for love of the theater, and not for pay; and their acting is therefore less likely to be perfunctory. They are as a class far better educated than the usual Broadway actor, and so they more easily grasp the essential idea of art theater production. It is necessary to add that in most amateur companies there is a sprinkling of players with more or less professional experience. In other words, the average player in such a company as that at the Arts and Crafts Theater does not come to the director as raw material. If he paradoxically needs an actor with the professional trick, to "carry" a scene, one is at hand; and if he wants the sincerity, the fresh charm and the intelligence of amateurs with a stage sense, he is likely to be over-supplied. In every American city there is this two-fold source: first, a group of intelligent, if untrained, amateurs who at least have a feeling for stage work; and second, a group of men and women with professional experience, who have left the stage to marry and settle down, or because they found life in the commercial theater uncongenial.

Perhaps the weightiest argument *against* the use of amateur players is that they cannot be depended upon for continuous work throughout the season. Family, business and social obligations may call them from the theater at critical moments. There is also a reasonable limit to the number of performances they can be asked to give in any one month, thus limiting the theater to occasional productions. By casting plays with one group the first month and utilizing a different group the second, and alternating as necessary, a regular schedule of say one week's productions each month can be counted on. But the fact remains that it will be impossible to take the final step toward the establishment of an art theater playing a continuous season without adopting a system under which the actors are paid. It is well to remember just here that many of the progressive theaters in Europe started with scattered performances.

What is it that distinguishes amateur actors from professionals? The original connotation of the word "amateur," of one who loves his work, must not be overlooked. The true amateur of the theater is the man or woman who acts for love of the art, and not primarily as a means of support. There can be no hard and fast line drawn, with the amateurs grouped on one side because they do not receive pay, and the professionals on the other because they are financially reimbursed for their appearances. It is rather a matter of the spirit in which one approaches the work. To my mind the Chicago Little Theater company was distinctly amateur—I say so in praise and not in disparagement. Despite the fact that the players received a small wage, they were held together primarily by a passion for the art of the theater. There was no temptation for them to become mere time-servers, for them to stoop to the commercial-professional's vice of learning the tricks that will bring the most money. Toward the end they had passed the early stages of amateurism, so that their work for a cause was both recognized and stabilized by the payment of a small monetary return; they seemed on the road to the best sort of professionalism, in which service to art is rewarded by a reasonable means to living. But they remained amateurs in spirit.

In paying his players Maurice Browne avoided the disadvantages implied in Sam Hume's theory that a progressive theater can obtain better results with the best unpaid amateurs than with the sort of professional it can afford to employ. When he was able to pay, he did not turn to the professional market, but continued with his amateurs. While he did not build up a company that was ideal, he made such progress in attaining coördination and unity of mood in acting that his opinion concerning amateurs is worth quoting:

"Professional actors and actresses, all of them incidentally once amateurs themselves, are carefully trained in certain stage-conventions, which after a time become second nature to them; these conventions are different from the new stage conventions which the leaders of the Art Theater movement are inventing, and therefore those trained in them are not directly helpful to such leaders, just as a man trained in classics is not directly helpful to a bridge builder; their uses are different. And, just as a bridge builder would sooner have for pupil a boy without any training than a boy with a training alien to his own, so the director of an Art Theater prefers to have players without any training (i. e., amateurs) than players trained in an alien convention. Moreover, the professional, so-called, in any walk of life, usually works primarily for money, while the amateur, so-called, that is to say the volunteer, works primarily for love of the work."

It is well to remind ourselves just here that both the theater of the Irish Players and the Moscow Art Theater had their beginnings in amateur organizations. By way of further light on the subject, let me quote Gilmor Brown, in regard to the Pasadena Community Playhouse:

"During the first season, a nucleus of paid players was retained. For minor parts, amateurs were called in. The result was unsatisfactory. An entirely non-professional basis was adopted the next year and has been maintained ever since. Experienced actors are not excluded; on the contrary, their coöperation is welcomed. But they always play on a volunteer basis in the Pasadena Community Playhouse, and the majority of all casts are amateurs."

Then let Frederic McConnell speak as representative of the group who mix paid "staff" actors and pure amateurs. His organization, of course, is the best example at the moment of an institutional theater which has outgrown practically every evidence of its amateur beginnings and is just arriving at the position of a full-fledged art theater—with an ideal building under construction, a permanent subscription audience, and a record of ninety-three plays already produced, including Shakespeare, Marlowe, Wilde, Shaw, Synge, Dunsany, Chesterton, Bottomley, Ibsen, Dostoievsky, Schnitzler, Heiberg, Echegaray, Pirandello, Vildrac, Galsworthy, Capek, d'Annunzio and O'Neill. In *Theater Arts Magazine* he writes:

"A production staff of seven people trained and experienced in the work of our type of theater provides a nucleus around which the theater in its many sided activity may function. This staff includes elements of stage direction, acting and production. Each member performs the duties for which he is specifically trained, but the staff works as a single unit in pushing through a particularly difficult project. This marked unity of effort has helped to give authority to whatever artistic policy we have elected to pursue. It has been the Director's principal aid in achieving and maintaining the real stage ensemble, which is of paramount importance in the theater.

"For six seasons a more or less fixed group has been acting together in a varied and distinctive repertory. This succession of ensemble playing has produced a technic and a spirit which, although not definable or recognizable under the criterion of the professional stage, is of special and intrinsic value to the Playhouse itself. Twenty people comprise this group of players. They, with the staff actors, are the front line of our stage ensemble. They have come up through the various struggles of the institution and were the first to respond to the ideal that playing was not for the sake of personal gratification and the release of personal emotion, but for the projection of dramatic values through the medium of the stage. The heavy increase in performances and production and the attendant impress of rehearsal has stimulated their interest rather than discouraged it. To this group the spirit of ensemble has come naturally and has made it possible for us to achieve a drama where the entity of self is lost in the entity of character. As time goes on and technical facility is added to our present spiritual equipment we should have all the elements of the perfect ensemble. Much of this technical facility is stimulated by the presence of competent staff actors and as the theater grows this staff will be increased. It is also important to observe that in a theater built from and around an ensemble, the trained actor will find the real opportunity for the development and exhibition of his powers. The combination of ensemble and repertory conveys to him the inevitable and inter-relating truths of subordination and dominance."

Bernard Shaw, by the way, makes the distinction not between amateurs and professionals, but between "artists" and "the trade."

Another perplexing circumstance is added by the action of Broadway managers in offering professional contracts to little theater actors who happen under their notice. It is reported that when the Dallas Little Theater company carried away the prize from the 1924 Little Theater Tournament in New York, two of the players carried away offers of employment in Broadway shows. Frederick Koch complains of similar "tampering" with his amateurs. Naturally the business producer believes that he is doing the beginner a great favor by offering such professional employment; whereas the little theater director looks at the offers with alarm, as unethical and as a danger to well-trained repertory artists. We shall doubtless hear a great deal more of this during the next ten years. Perhaps it will become ethical for a member of the Cleveland Playhouse Company, say, or of the Garden Players, to jump his implied contract at home and go to full professional service at the beckoning of the Theater Guild or some other "regular" art theater; whereas desertion to Mr. Woods or Mr. Shubert will be considered reprehensible and in bad taste. In any case, I think it will not be so long before an organization like the Guild will have its scouts out informally, looking for likely recruits from the little theaters, to its "studios" if not to its regular companies.

VI

Of the position of the actor under the ultimate art theater I shall have something to say in a later chapter. But here I wish to point out two facts: in the commercial theater the degradation from the position of artist to the position of a shopkeeper with a line of goods to sell has resulted from an organization under which the actor was relieved of responsibility and deprived of direct interest in his company's doings; second, the loss of the best traditions of his art was due to the long-run and circuit systems, under which the player was denied opportunity to play varied rôles, and the leisure and incentive necessary to make him a student in the broader sense. These faults will be corrected in the art theater, where the actor will again become a coöperative partner, if not in ownership, at least to a degree in the artistic administration of the theater. He will be employed under annual contract, with certain pension rights and proprietary interests accruing with added years of service. The theater will be his in a very true sense, and it will secure to him those advantages of permanency, of breadth of opportunity, of versatile repertory of parts, and of balance of work and recreation, which are necessary to his finest development.

VII

The economic position of the professional actor has been very much improved during the last ten years, due chiefly to the success of the so-called "actors' union": the Actors' Equity Association. Even before the actors' strike in 1919, when the producing managers were routed in a merry battle, the Association had made headway in bettering conditions and standardizing contracts. The chief gains have been in limiting the number of weeks a player may be expected to rehearse without remuneration; enforcing a minimum payment after a long rehearsal period, even if the play closes almost immediately after opening; securing to the actor a proportionate additional salary for extra performances; cleaning up intolerable conditions on stages and in dressing rooms; bringing back to New York or other point of departure the "broke" and stranded members of traveling companies abandoned by irresponsible managers; and enforcing contractual obligations on the part of both actor and producer. Among the other gains made by the A. E. A. and its twelve thousand members, the one that is least often mentioned, perhaps, but most important here is the new foundation it gives to the player for self-respect as an artist. As a member of a solidly organized and respected group, he is able to join in coördinate action for the establishment of dignified institutional theaters, where the actor may be a creative partner in production, and not merely a temporarily hired and time-serving helper.

A sound economic status for the artist is the healthiest condition for the development of an art. It seems to me incumbent, therefore, upon the actors of our maturing progressive theaters, as soon as they reach the standing of professional players, to join in association with those who have already stabilized the profession and who are constantly working toward more equitable conditions for everybody concerned. Because repertory art theaters are so little known in the America of to-day, there are doubtless provisions of the Equity contract that must be modified to further the growth of the institutional theater. But the present officers of the A. E. A. have fortunately shown themselves not only wise in their efforts to protect their members, but forward-looking and solicitous for every project that tends to improve the theater as a whole. Official actordom can be counted upon as an ally in any venture that is essentially and unselfishly for the good of the art of the theater.

CHAPTER VII

THE QUESTION OF PLAYS

Of course, any *good* play is material for the art theater. It is equally true that every producer on Broadway will avow that he is seeking good plays. The dividing line between good and bad, or even between good and so-so, is not easily placed—or recognized. Mr. Belasco apparently believes that *Ladies of the Evening* is a good play. Yet you would not catch Miss Helburn of the Theater Guild or Mr. Digges of the Actors' Theater having anything to do with the production of it. Nor would you catch Mr. Belasco producing *John Ferguson* or *Processional* or *Candida* or *Rosmersholm*. But Mr. Belasco or Mr. Ames or the Guild or the Actors' Theater might produce *Anna Christie* or *Sumurun* or *As You Like It* or *The Blue Bird*.

About all one can say is that there is a vague distinction between what is a typical play for a serious organization and what is a play for a purely commercial manager, and that some examples qualify in both types; and insofar as the commercial producer waxes serious or intelligent, he tends to invade the other field, and insofar as the organization feels that it must compete commercially, to pay the rent or to escape the reputation of being highbrow, it tends to pick a popular and negligible play now and then. The distinction is very much that vague one which divides literature from journalism.

Broadway, of course, is most often concerned with a journalistic product. It wants plays that are timely, direct, obviously written, sensational, with combined sentimentalism and pep. Topical. Snappy. The institutional theaters in general are concerned with something less obviously appealing, something with a residue value after the emotional shock or the laughter has gone, something opening up a contemplative vista or revealing a new understanding of life or leaving the spectator in a mood of beauty. (One might as well try to define art!)

I

Perhaps it is true that the really great play, the universally important play, beautifully staged, appeals to both audiences. But let us emphasize the dividing line, for our purposes here. Let us take it that the commercial-manager plays run true to the journalistic type; and that the really advanced and matured art theater tends to a specialized type of serious play. Then the question arises: shall the American embryo art theaters immediately set up an advanced ideal of play which will cut them off from the patronage of any but moderate-sized or small audiences? Or shall they compromise by mixing the journalistic product with occasional attempts at the recognizably artistic? Or shall they adopt a standard of play that finds its level where the two sorts meet—never too "advanced" and never too clearly vulgar? In short, where, between the art ideal and the amusement ideal, shall the average little theater that aspires to be an art theater set its standard? What is an art theater conscience? And how elastic?

There are those who refuse to compromise. But for many of those who have been in the fight it has seemed necessary, if they would exist at all, if they objected to going out of existence until such time as an inspired millionaire staked them to pursue the higher ideal, audience or no audience, to recognize two goals: one the immediate establishment of theaters progressive enough in choice of plays and methods of staging to be clearly steps beyond the commercial average and toward a higher ideal; and the other an ultimate ideal of absolute art, with no concession to supposed popular demand. I think that to-day we have progressed beyond the point where any real idealist of the new theater would put the matter quite so rawly. But it is worth while to analyze the compromise attitude dispassionately.

II

Sam Hume, in explaining the success of the first season at the Arts and Crafts Theater, laid great stress on the fact that he fitted the series of plays to the demands of the community. "We were dependent," he said, "on a certain group of theater-goers for our existence. We were careful, therefore, not to hit over the heads of that group. It happened to be an unusually intelligent class, but it was not interested in the esoteric and precious material which certain little theaters affect. We were able to choose dignified, worth-while plays, and we tried to produce them according to the best ideals of staging. But we avoided plays of very limited appeal. We made good because we did not keep too far ahead of our audiences, because we did not try unduly to force the movement for better art in the theater."

An analysis of that season's bills at the Arts and Crafts Theater shows that only six of the nineteen plays produced were at all unusual or specialized in appeal. One of these appeared on each of the six programs of the season—which indicates that when Hume wished to try something a little "advanced" on his audiences, he sandwiched it between things of more obvious appeal. While trying to educate his community to a taste for something different from the current fare of the commercial theater, he stayed close enough to that in general so that the audiences would not be driven away by the strangeness of his offerings.

As a whole it is not a list that would do credit to a mature art theater. Plays of a passing vogue or distinctly light in appeal are in the majority. On the other hand, it is a list that bespeaks a clear advance beyond the standards of the commercial theater. It is a working illustration of Hume's theory: keep ahead of business standards, but never go so far into untried fields or toward the art of particularized appeal, that the audiences of the moment will be antagonized.

Scenes from Lenormand's *The Failures* as produced by the New York Theater Guild, in settings by Lee Simonson. (Photographs by Francis Bruguiere.)

III

Considered by no other standard than the type of play produced, the Chicago Little Theater, of all the widely known projects, has been incomparably the closest American approach to an art theater. Its productions came measurably near the art that appeals to a highly cultivated audience. An analysis of its list of plays shows that Maurice Browne preferred to strike direct to the ultimate goal as he saw it. He refused to compromise for the sake of conciliating audiences or critics.

In the five seasons at Chicago the proportion of poetic and fantastic plays was not considerably greater than at Detroit. But the selection was more revolutionary, including such names as Euripides (in Gilbert Murray's remarkable translation), Yeats, and Synge; and original productions of plays by American authors were made with the particular object of finding a typical art theater type of play. In the non-poetic or less poetic groups, moreover, the Chicago Little Theater list tends far more to the serious, is freer from mere "fillers" than is the Detroit or any later list. Ibsen, Shaw, Schnitzler, Hankin, Strindberg, Gibson, Wilde—these are names which bespeak a preoccupation with what is too dignified, too thoughtful and too true to figure in the average theater's announcements.

It would be idle to claim that devotion to a theory does not beget very great advantages artistically. One must admire any artist who sets up an ideal, and then, although realizing that it is far ahead of the public, pursues it uncompromisingly, in the face of apathy, and in spite of criticism both fair and unfair. And there are definite advantages to the particular theater and to the art theater movement in general. Thus the Chicago Little Theater will always be known as a pioneer in the search for a characteristic art theater technique. It aided the whole movement through its pioneering activities and it gained a lasting distinction thereby.

The material disadvantages of such a policy are evident, particularly when the Chicago Little Theater history is examined beside that of the Arts and Crafts Theater. The Detroit play-list was built on the assumption that one must speak at first in a language which sizable audiences can understand, and then develop the community with the theater as the artistic standards are raised. The system worked admirably so far as holding satisfactory audiences was concerned. The Chicago Little Theater, on the other hand, gained a reputation for a restricted appeal. It became known as a theater for a specialized audience, if not for a cult, and this militated against its wider acceptance as a community venture, and cut off needed income. Devotion to an ideal estranged the institution from its public. To put it rawly, the Chicago Little Theater was too artistic to succeed financially at that stage of American culture.

IV

There is, perhaps, a middle course. One has come

to abhor the old saying that "a play must please the public"—because so much pandering has been done under the shadow of that banner. One may believe, however, that the whole art of the theater is to a certain extent conditioned upon public acceptance. It is possible to be too ruthless in one's disregard for the preferences of a fairly intelligent audience. I don't mean that any progressive group can consciously set out to please the average intelligence of even a picked audience—for "pleasing" as a business is narrowing and deadening. But don't be bull-headed about feeding what you consider "high art" in unrelieved doses; have catholicity of taste, have variety, unbend to light comedy and the topical play occasionally.

In short, the art theater should keep ahead of its audiences, but without going to the ruthless extreme. I don't know where to find a better example of the "high middle" course than in the production list of the Cleveland Playhouse. During the last four years forty-eight plays have been presented, nine one-acts and thirty-nine full-length. Of these no fewer than thirty-eight are such that no highly serious theorist about the drama could possibly take exception to them: Shakespeare, Marlowe, Ibsen, Shaw, Synge, Schnitzler, Wiers-Jenssen, Ervine, Pirandello, Echegaray and the like. Among the other ten are two plays by a local dramatist, a spectacle, two or three serious plays that I don't know well enough to classify, and—here's the point—an occasional excursion into material as light and unpretentious as Harry Wagstaff Gribble's *March*

Hares and the insubstantial comedies of Clare Kummer and A. A. Milne.

The Provincetown Players have achieved something of the same sort of average. In their early days they did it by accepting native plays of the most serious sort and of the lightest—but always with a standard of intelligence that ruled out pure hokum, and farce without literary or satiric value; and in their later reincarnation, by playing such very special and rarefied works as Strindberg's *The Spook Sonata* and Hasenclever's *Beyond* against stylized revivals of such onetime favorites as *Fashion* and *Patience*—the whole insured against loss by constant return to the safety of Eugene O'Neill's serious plays, that may be said to appeal to both art theater audiences and a larger, merely sensation-loving audience.

The Theater Guild has never compromised in the matter of usualness—one goes to its productions certain that it won't be a case of boredom by the obvious or the outworn; but its course might be called middling in respect to choice of plays for lasting and universal values. The list through seven seasons shows that the directors have a flair for the latest artistic novelty; and at times they have brought in very fine plays that all other producers seemed afraid to touch. But the direction of their compromise has been toward those intelligent plays that would draw through sex-interest and a daring sophistication if all other appeals failed.

Perhaps the most interesting repertory at an American theater, from the viewpoint of variety, is that of the Pasadena Community Playhouse. It cannot be called a compromise theater in general, for there are eleven Shakespearean productions in the list (has any other American organization done so many?), and there is more than usual of Sheridan, Wilde, Moliere, Congreve, etc., and a generous sprinkling of the most "special" moderns, Strindberg, Yeats, Andreyev, Kennedy, Maeterlinck, besides the usual Shaw, Barrie and Galsworthy. But the surprising thing is the number of typical Broadway best-sellers that are sandwiched between: Winchell Smith, W. C. deMille, Rachel Crothers, Edward Knoblock, the Nugents, Edward Peple, Montague Glass, George Kelly. Here is a double aim of providing an art theater and reflecting Broadway for a community to which Broadway seldom comes. Certainly it is not a "high art" list of plays—but with many of the most unusual of items of serious drama in it.

When I talk of compromise in play choice, it is clear that in my own mind I know what *I* would include in an art theater's repertory, and what I would exclude. Perhaps ideals and all questions of "compromise" and "opportunism" are so largely matters of personal judgment and taste that I have no real right to criticise the Pasadena group or the Guild or any other, even by implication, for its play list. There is one department, however—the classics—where one can be on fairly safe ground.

V

Every large city should be able to see the classics of the theater as readily as it can see examples of Rembrandt, El Greco, Whistler, Cezanne, at its art gallery. We are bound to have, indeed, playhouses corresponding to the dignified subventioned theaters of France and Germany. How many productions of Shakespeare were there in first-class American theaters this season or last? There are approximately three thousand performances of Shakespeare's plays in Germany annually: not in a few productions, but in every one of his plays, at scores of theaters, all over the country. What does Chicago or St. Louis or Boston or San Francisco see of Sophocles, Euripides, Marlowe, Congreve, Moliere, Goldoni, Schiller? The residents of those cities are likely to remember them, if at all, from the productions they once saw in Stuttgart or Dresden or Moscow or Paris or Vienna, when they went to Europe on their wedding trips. Unless, indeed, they happened on to Euripides in some sabbatical performance at the Greek Theater in Berkeley, or Moliere at a French Society Centenary, or a Harvard Stadium production by a visiting English director—or possibly at scratch performances by strolling open-air players. As for a home for the classics in America, and regular professional performances, we are entirely innocent.

How long, then, will America continue to send students across the Atlantic to see the finest of the world's plays adequately presented? How long will America leave the stay-at-homes without any possibility of viewing a wide range of dramatic classics even in a lifetime? New York and Chicago could certainly each support one theater playing only or mainly the masterpieces of other times. It will take ten years to build the repertory of such an institution to maturity—but it will be worth both the time and the subsidy.

Personally I happen to be more interested in a theater playing contemporary works as well. We need in most of our art theaters the encouragement to native authors which dignified production will give. A theater is likely to keep the spirit of youth, or creativeness, if its repertory is wide. One recollects that the Comédie Française has been too narrowly national to serve the best interests of French dramatic art. The list of plays at an American art theater should doubtless include classic and modern drama, the work of both foreign and native playwrights, and plays in all modes: poetic, romantic, realistic, expressionistic.

To return to the classics, however, it is doubtful whether the American theatergoing public realizes how glorious an experience their revival can afford; how *living* they are if adequately presented. When they are brought to us now in an infrequent performance, they are too seldom satisfying in a complete way. They have been produced as cut to fit a Broadway star, and smothered with spectacular Broadway scenery; and they have been revived more intelligently, but amateurishly and archæologically, at the colleges. To say that the public will not patronize them in their finest embodiment is merest speculation. The public has had no chance to judge. Under art theater treatment, with the poetry brought out, and with dramatic story, acting and setting properly inter-related and stylized, they can be made to live again for modern audiences. As tastes of what they may mean, some of us remember Margaret Anglin's company in the series at the Greek Theater, Berkeley, and the stylized performances of the Chicago Little Theater. We remember, too, how William Poel took one of the least interesting of Elizabethan comedies and made it appeal to American audiences merely by his *manner* of production—which he claimed was the Elizabethan manner—convincing many progressives that if "the public does not like classics," it is the method of staging that is at fault.

Walter Hampden has several times made the effort to establish a permanent company, playing a repertory of classics almost exclusively, and no doubt he will accomplish it before many seasons have passed. Two years ago he leased a New York playhouse and announced a repertory plan; but he ran into a great monetary success with *Cyrano de Bergerac*, and abandoned all other considerations to make capital while the golden sun shone. Other repertory projects have gone the same way. One remembers only too well that celebrated and barbed conundrum: "When is a repertory theater not a repertory theater?—When it is a success." But sooner or later there will be groups that have interest enough and faith enough not to be tempted by the financial returns from the long run of a "find." And Walter Hampden is not likely to let his defection from the repertory idea prove permanent. His interest in the theater is too fundamental, his attitude too sincere, to permit his desertion to any primarily commercial pursuit.

Shakespeare and the other Elizabethan dramatists are as much the classics of the American theater as Moliere, Corneille and Racine are of the French. And so the American art theater will most often turn to Shakespeare and his contemporaries for their revivals. But the best things from the French, German, Spanish and other languages will find place also, if we are wise. And let me repeat, audiences will accept them. In drama, as in music, one's taste improves with experience of the best. Appreciation follows opportunity.

VI

Of modern plays, it would be unwise to suggest that any type beyond crass melodrama and empty farce should be looked upon with suspicion in the art theater. Who is to say, for example, where the emotionally effective and legitimate drama of thought is to be divided from the propaganda play? And who is to mark a boundary between mere naturalism and inspired realism? Some people think that it is possible to divide intelligent drama into two classes, the play of beauty and the play of ideas; and they would have the art theater concerned only with the play of beauty. They would put the whole realistic school, including Ibsen, Shaw, Galsworthy, Schnitzler and many another, outside the pale. Not so fast, my worthies!

No doubt a general distinction can be made between a substantially poetic group of dramatists and a typically realistic or literal group: the one relying chiefly on literary, imaginative and romantic appeal, and the other, through its intensive observation of life, bringing a more direct emotional reaction coupled with a stimulus to thought. And there can be no doubt that to keep a wholesome balance we must have a great deal more of poetic drama than the business theater has offered. American theatergoers have been starved for imaginative drama for years. Yeats, Synge, Dunsany, Hauptmann, Maeterlinck, Pirandello, d'Annunzio—these are names that are likely to have large place in art theater repertories, certainly larger than any business producer would grant possible.

But it is necessary also to recognize that our immature progressive theaters, in the broader view, have hardly more than caught up with the best phases of realism. We are in the period of the German and Russian advanced theaters of twenty years ago. What else does it mean that we are having "cycles" of Ibsen and Shaw? (My guess is that Schnitzler will be next.) Our theater is still digging back into life.

I happen to be one of those who believe that in the ultimate estimate of history the realistic movement will seem far less significant than it does to most critics to-day. I believe that even the form of our stage will change from the present proscenium-frame, peephole affair to a formal architectural platform and lightable space, and that the fourth-wall convention will be abandoned. But the realistic drama is still a very great part of the theatrical expression of the times. America has never caught up with the masters of the immediate past—masters of a minor efflorescence, but integral to the world activity and the theater of this time. And so, while my greater and ultimate allegiance is to a stage of the post-Shaw era, I know that the American art theater will for the present be largely sustained by Ibsen, Tolstoy, Shaw, Barker, Galsworthy and other realist-intellectual playwrights. For most of us, in this age of extensive half-learning and vicarious living, ideas are among the most interesting and important things in life. So on with the idea-play!

Of signs of the coming of a later type of play, suited to a later type of stage, there are many. Anyone who has read manuscripts for a progressive manager or a progressive producing group knows how many of the younger playwrights of America have felt the influence of the thing called Expressionism. The trend is toward the emotional-crisis play as against the thought play, toward intensity of feeling as against likeness to outward life and truthfulness of detail, toward looseness of technique as against formula. There are already near-masters in the style: Kaiser, Hasenclever, Toller—the last being author of *Masse-Mensch*, which stands in my mind (as played at the *Volksbühne* in Berlin, and not in New York) as the type-example of the expressionistic method, unrealistic, apparently unconventional in form, intensely dynamic, extraordinarily moving emotionally, a hurried series of crises. There are American dramatists utilizing the style too; most notably John Howard Lawson, whose *Roger Bloomer* and *Processional* are finely original and genuinely emotional and theatric. Toward that sort of non-naturalistic theatricalism and intensification of life the road to the future seems to lie. And any progressive theater must have an eye to that immediate future as well as to the immediate neglected past.

It should be added that there are types of dramatic expression suited to organizational and coöperative production and practically impossible in the ordinary theater. I am thinking particularly of the so-called religious play—where a spiritual oneness is a requirement in the acting and direction. I can think of no existing American theater organization mature enough and interested enough to develop a spiritually expressive original drama of the sort; but I feel certain that it will come, as the right circumstances and creative ability come together. In another field, that of creative dance-drama, the Neighborhood Playhouse in New York has developed its own original type of dance-play and method of expression. The same group has brought its burlesque-revue, the *Grand Street Follies*, to the point of being an annual red-letter event in the calendar of New York's fixed theatrical attractions. In one way and another, incidentally, burlesque and revue have swallowed up more than their fair share of the talent, genius and creativeness of the present generation in the American theater.

VII

One other important consideration must enter into the choice of plays: the proportion of native to foreign works. Just as in the matter of classics, the list should be open to the widest possible selection from the contemporary drama of other countries. The best should be taken from European dramatists, not only because for some years to come their best is likely to be better than our best, but also because we need to study their drama for an understanding of those universal principles which will some day underlie our own—and because the art theater building is to be the home of sheer dramatic beauty whatever its origin. Just here it is well to remind ourselves that the most intensely national drama of modern times, the Irish, found its finest expression in the works of two men of international culture and training. Yeats began his dramatic career in London, and knew well both the English and the French theaters before he became interested in the project at Dublin; and Synge had spent many years on the Continent previous to his connection with the Irish National Theater. An understanding internationalism is the soundest basis for an inspiring nationalism.

But while opening our theaters so freely to foreign artists, we must remember that the future development of American drama depends largely upon the present encouragement offered native playwrights. We have seen how the commercialization of the playhouse deprived the aspiring playwright of all laboratory facilities. While we cannot afford to lower art theater standards to those of the laboratory and purely experimental theaters, we shall do well to recognize that every schedule of productions should make room for a certain number of native pieces. The knowledge that such theaters await plays of merit spurs dramatists to do a serious sort of work, which would never be called forth by the demands of the business playhouse. The Abbey Theater so inspired a generation of Irish writers that an entire new dramatic literature resulted.

It is not probable that we shall have a national drama in the Irish sense, or even in the French sense. As a federated group-nation, without a single art capital—New York is hardly more than a center of business art—we cannot expect to have the intense national feeling which would bring forth a deeply characteristic body of drama. It is more likely that we shall have a sectional drama, of New England, of the Middle West, of the Far West, and this collectively may have a definite note which can be recognized as American. If so, it is even more imperative that the sectional art theaters provide the native playwright with facilities for staging really meritorious work.

In other countries playwrights have sometimes led revolts in the theater. In America the struggle for a better stage has found its leaders in other groups. The great mass of established American dramatists are tied to the business machine; and so long as they get a fair share of the profits thereof, they feel no urge

The formal stage at the Théâtre du Vieux Colombier in Paris, as set for a scene in *The Brothers Karamazov.* From a drawing by Robert Edmond Jones. (By courtesy of Harcourt, Brace and Company.)

to help foster a different sort of theater. The men who are writing plays which they submit to the progressive producing groups are largely the youngsters who are just beginning. And an extraordinarily promising lot they are, too. Any reader for an organizational theater will testify that he receives a remarkable number of scripts that are marked by sincerity of handling, original material and a sense of characterization. A great many of these just miss being fine producible plays, and the average quality augurs extremely well for the future. What is most generally lacking, perhaps, is a "sense of the theater"—theatrical fluency, stageworthiness. It is again the lack of the laboratory during the last quarter-century that has created the fault.

The Actors' Theater tried for two years the experiment of producing practically nothing but new American plays. It brought to Broadway eight original native works (all full-length) out of its first eleven productions. But the critics and the public allowed nothing for the fact that here was an attempt to aid the American dramatist by putting forward his works in the finest possible productions. At the beginning of the third year the organization was forced to recognize that it could not secure five new native plays each year that warranted the large expenditure necessary for full professional production in competition with the commercial producers. No doubt many more than five worthy ones are produced each year, but no single producer or group can hope to secure that many. The Actors' Theater abandoned the policy as impractical. It found further that the playwrights who submitted plays to a progressive and co-operative organization were seldom the old established authors whose names already carried advertising weight. A poll of the leading dramatists, indeed, revealed that many of them were under contract to commercial producers for present and future output; and the most successful ones had first and second options out. Not that the progressive organizations generally will care to produce primarily the work of the present established playwrights; there will be more profit for them in cultivating a new generation of writers for the stage. But the Actors' Theater had elected to play the game in a leased theater on Broadway, and felt that it needed the prestige of recognized dramatists' names at least occasionally.

A fact noted by the organization during the last year is this: after the excellent productions of *Candida* and *The Wild Duck*, which brought the group its widest advertising and crystallized its reputation for a very high standard of acting, mounting and directing, a certain number of the old-line dramatists came voluntarily to offer plays which either had failed to interest the regular managers or seemed too "special" for any but a progressive outfit. Certainly an institutional theater in New York maintaining a standard near that of the Moscow Art Theater or the Berlin State Theater would, after its initial period, attract by virtue of its production standard many of the finest native dramas written by contemporary authors.

An organization called the Dramatists' Theater has been operating in New York for two years. All its productions have been of native plays, and one, Lewis Beach's *The Goose Hangs High*, attained a considerable success. But this is not an institutional theater in the accepted sense; it is, indeed, hardly more than a producing partnership of several playwrights. It has no subscription audience, and therefore does not bind itself to offer any given number of plays in a season. It has offered three productions on Broadway in two years, in direct competition with the purely commercial managers, but with better-than-average plays.

There have been little theaters established particularly for the purpose of fostering the development of native dramatists. The most important example is the Provincetown Players. This group would have a creditable record of discovery and aid even without Eugene O'Neill. It afforded a laboratory stage for many an important writer just breaking into the dramatic field. In giving O'Neill his chance, it ushered into the American theater the man who has become the one internationally significant native playwright. The Washington Square Players also did pioneer work in opening a channel for home-made drama, a generous majority of their plays being of native authorship. This partiality for the American product was not one of the inheritances of the Theater Guild from the Washington Square group. The Guild has, indeed, been scored again and again for its neglect of the native author. It has made thirty-eight productions, and the vehicles were American in only six cases.

For three seasons the Beechwood Players at Scarborough, New York, have followed the policy of producing almost exclusively new full-length American plays. Occasionally they have turned up a script with exceptional values; and they have served the cause well by affording a number of authors the opportunity to see their works acted before audiences. Once in a while a play has seemed so much a "discovery" when staged at the Beechwood Theater that it graduated to Broadway; and at the other extreme the organization has given performances to several plays only to discover in the final result just why the New York producers had wisely rejected them. On the whole, the group has probably afforded its audiences entertainment just about as good as the average established at little theaters with professional directors elsewhere. And it has had the broader interest of discovery and aid to native writers. Incidentally the group has what is a very close approach to an ideal little theater plant, and it has occasionally acted a play in a manner superior to the later professional production on Broadway.

Perhaps the most striking example of direct aid to native playwriting at present is Frederick Koch's work with the Carolina Playmakers. His little theater group is a laboratory class in playwriting, acting and production. His "company" produces only locally written plays on native themes, and it has been so successful in finding audiences for its offerings that there is prospect of a second, graduate, semi-professional company in addition to the original laboratory class. Just how far this experiment will serve creatively the wider national theater, the collective art theaters of America, it is impossible to judge in these early days. Several emulators of Professor Koch have started similar work in other states. It is hardly too much to expect some inland O'Neill to find his start with a "Playmaker" group. Meantime North Carolina village audiences enjoy dramatized tales of their own locale—while New York, Cleveland, and Chicago take their progressive dramatic fare with an exotic flavor, in the reflected light of European culture.

To return to the question of the proportion of American and foreign work that one of our near-art theaters might fairly be expected to maintain in its productions under present circumstances, I think that a half-and-half average would work well both ways—in maintaining breadth and in bringing out native talent. I know that this is asking an advantage for the American author, for I realize fully that the really fine drama by a native playwright is only too rare, and even more difficult for any but the best-known group to secure. But I want just a little prejudice for the native playwright at this stage of development, a tendency to put his fairly good play on the boards in preference to a foreign work that is just a little better. Through his experience of the stage this time he is likely to equal his European rival next time.

I believe, moreover, that the development of a really large body of important American drama is only a matter of a decade or two. Already we have material not unworthy of an art theater's repertory. One might start the list with a few works which no one would challenge, such as *The Yellow Jacket* and *The Poor Little Rich Girl.* Then there are many plays which, while doubtless subject to minority objection, are well worthy of revival—poetic works like Percy MacKaye's *The Scarecrow* and Mrs. Marks' *The Piper*, and more realistic plays like Charles Kenyon's *Kindling*, Augustus Thomas' *As a Man Thinks*, and O'Neill's *Beyond the Horizon.* But I have more faith in the importance of dramas to be written by such comparative newcomers as Susan Glaspell, Cloyd Head, Sidney Howard, Dan Totheroh, Knowles Entrikin, Martin Flavin and John Howard Lawson.

VIII

The American art theater will, of course, be a repertory theater. It will doubtless modify the repertory plan of such institutions as the Comédie Française, retaining a certain latitude in the length of run of a successful new play. Its economic position may be such that at first it will have to keep an occasional success on the boards for several weeks. But it should never offer less than a certain scheduled number of plays in a season; and it must gradually build up a group of plays for revival, covering classic and modern. Only thus can it fulfill its true function as an institution serving a community in relation to theater art as the art gallery serves it in relation to painting and sculpture. Repertory organization brings its serious problems, particularly where there is competition with the commercial long-run system. But only through its advantages, its method of conserving the best plays out of the theaters of the past and present, can we hope to combat effectively the narrowing influence of the business theater.

CHAPTER VIII

THE QUESTION OF STAGE SETTINGS

AFTER experiencing some little difficulty, if not embarrassment, in trying to balance fairly the claims of the beginning, the hampered American playwright and actor and director, against the achievement of the experienced and world-recognized artists of the European art theaters, I note a sense of pleasure in coming to a chapter wherein the American worker is right up at the top in full-flowered achievement as well as in promise for the future. For our mature art theater, we have more talented stage designers than we can readily make use of; and two or three of them are experienced men of a fecund imagination and versatile practice which place them among the world's best dozen in this field.

Because the ideal of the art theater, as understood by its earliest workers, demanded that every element going to make up a production should contribute to the creation of a single mood, it was necessary that the older methods of stage setting be discarded. The carelessly unnatural, the literal, and the spectacular modes of scene-making had to give way before a stage craft which found its first principles in the synthetic ideal: imaginative invention, contributive expressiveness, atmospheric beauty, subordination of specific interest to creation of mood.

Ten years ago the Americans had no mature art theaters wherein to experiment or prove their talents. The painters, architects and other designers in the visual arts, who had become enamored of the stage, accepted the next best thing. They turned to the little theaters. They apparently descended on the little theater in hordes. Whether American playwrights failed or not, whether amateur actors gave only half-substance to the dramatist's intention, it was an exceptional little theater that didn't have adequate, pretty, novel and at times beautiful stage pictures during the last five years. Some of the best of the stage designers, moreover, long ago graduated to more professional pastures, were hired by the business-producers to dress up the shows on Broadway—so that to-day the settings of a year's crop of plays in New York are probably more intelligently designed for their purpose, more lovely in their fullness of color, their atmospheric lighting and their lavish richness than any similar group of productions in any other city of the world (Berlin papers please *don't* copy!). At any rate, the finest group-talent in the American theater to-day is to be found in the little company known as "the younger decorators"—(they squirm under that phrase: decoration as such has quite gone out, and everybody is for the architectural stage, space, the actor emphasized by light, disappearing backgrounds, and variety through multiple levels and designed movement). Certainly one could not pick from among the directors, the playwrights or the actors a half-dozen men so efficient in their craft, so forward-looking in a sane way, so broadly visionary, so sensitive to world changes in the other arts and in the theater, as Robert Edmond Jones, Norman-Bel Geddes, Hermann Rosse, Lee Simonson, Woodman Thompson, Rollo Peters, Claude Bragdon. And one might with little compunction add James Reynolds, Cleon Throckmorton, Max Gorelik, Jo Mielziner, Livingston Platt, John Wenger, Frederick Jones, Donald Oenslager, and Ernest de Weerth. Even then one has not gone out of New York, nor included the veteran Viennese-American, Joseph Urban, unfortunately lost to the moving-picture factories. Out of the West, moreover, new names are heard, from which another Geddes or another Thompson may be added. It is well to recognize, of course, that these designers alone cannot make a new theater, and that our current stage, commercial and otherwise, is perhaps a bit over-rich with decoration, over-pictured. But it is very comforting to know that the visual side of staging will be excellently well cared for when we have a dozen or a half hundred developed professional art theaters.

I

In the bad old days, the stage setting was based on a literal transcription into paint, canvas and properties of certain facts set down in a playwright's stage directions. If doors were called for, doors were cut in walls, but with little regard for scale or for proportion of wall space to openings; and windows, mantels and other accessories were supplied as a builder might supply them without an architect's help. The result usually was literally and materially correct. If the designer wished to add something by way of decoration it was entirely in the nature of ornament stuck on. In other words, the designer of stage settings seldom made his scene spiritually true to the inner mood of the play, but only materially true to its practical demands; he seldom made it structurally decorative, but only built up something spectacular and decorative from his own standpoint, and very little related to the spiritual content of the drama. The methods used, moreover, were absurdly artificial, considering the naturalistic aims of the period. Supposedly wooden walls quaked at the slightest touch, broad landscapes wrinkled in the breeze, ships cast grotesque shadows on the sky, furniture was even painted on the walls, and the woodwork had painted lights and shadows that never matched the surrounding real light and shade. These and similar crudities were accepted as necessary accompaniments of the art of stage setting. It was not the artificiality of art—the conventionalized taking the place of the real—but the artificiality of incompetence.

The staging of a generation ago was so very bad that even some of the American managers revolted against it. David Belasco, with his passion for thoroughness, was particularly instrumental in giving a certain substantial illusion to the box-set interior, and eliminating the most grossly artificial features from exteriors. But this revolt was solely in the direction of naturalism. It did not start with the desire to bring the setting into closer harmony with the spirit of the play, but only with the object of making the scene more natural. It removed the worst absurdities of Nineteenth-Century staging; but in its later elaboration it provided distractions quite as foreign to the substance of the drama. In the pursuit of the natural, Belasco and others began to build scenes so finely imitative, so true to the surface appearances of life, that the audience often forgot the play in wonder at the photographic perfection of the setting.

The revolt of the artists, beginning with Craig and Appia, was against both the artificiality of the older theater and the naturalism of the Belasco group. The specific aim of the newly conceived stagecraft was to bring the setting into definite spiritual harmony with the play. Suggestion was substituted for imitation, creation of atmosphere was considered more important than indication of a definite locality, and the appeal of the setting was subordinated to the complete appeal of the production as a whole, by simplification and conventionalization. Where visual beauty was the aim of the dramatist and artist-director, the setting became a thing of beauty predicated upon the mood of the play; and its decorative quality grew out of skillful composition of line and mass, subtle use of color, and a system of lighting designed more for artistic expressiveness than for mere naturalness.

II

What the revolt came to, in practice, may legitimately be described in three general classifications. If one took all the work at all the art theaters, and of all the progressive designers named, one might conceivably find room for everything in these three divisions: the improved painters' settings, the plastic setting (naturalism simplified, made three-dimensional, and designed), and the stylistically conventionalized setting and formal stages.

I wish to write of the painter phase first because it can quickly be dismissed. Certain Russian designers have developed a wonderfully brilliant technique in painting scenery. They accept the old theater convention which said that an exterior setting must be done in painted perspective on canvas. In other words, they still consider the stage scene a glorified easel picture. Some of their settings are among the richest and most interesting of the creations masquerading under the name of the new stagecraft. But they really have nothing to do with the most typical phases of the new movement. They mark merely the perfection of a process that will never give absolute satisfaction in the theater, except in frankly artificial or "period" productions. They are infinitely better than the settings in the same method which used to fill all our theaters, because they are painted by artists instead of sign painters. But two points are to be noted about them: First, they employ naturalistic painted perspective in the backgrounds, and this will very seldom prove entirely satisfying on the stage; for no matter how cunningly the artist may work to hide all traces of the incongruity, there will always be a disillusioning difference between the real perspective of the foreground and the painted perspective at the back—and audiences will be less and less tolerant of this absurdity as they become trained in appreciation of the plastic, perspective-less method. And second, these artists are employing a purely *representative* method: instead of placing backgrounds and objects on the stage, or suggesting these things by concrete means, or omitting them altogether, they attempt to represent them by the illustrator's method, which properly has no place in any theater later than Pinero's time.

The painter, indeed, has proven himself inadequate to the tasks of the theater; and the designer for the stage of the future will need the training of architect, sculptor and interior decorator rather than that of the present-day painter—training in arrangement of abstract line and mass, form-organization, harmony of flat color-tones, and particularly an understanding of the stage as stage.

For my part, I believe that within not so very many years the painted-perspective background will be as clearly ridiculous and out-of-date in a stage production as the soliloquy and aside are in modern playwriting.*

* In my first edition of this book I said of this sentence: "I know that ninety-nine out of every hundred of the so-called artists on Broadway would call me crazy if I repeated that statement to them. But I do not base the contention on mere theorizing—although I was convinced of the soundness of the theory of plastic setting several years ago. I have seen both sorts in large and small, and the plastic is so far superior by every measurement that its time is sure to come. In at least two of the most progressive theaters in this country, the Arts and Crafts Theater in Detroit and the Los Angeles

III

The plastic method of setting, which has so largely replaced the painter's pictorial method in the progressive theaters of both Europe and America, implies primarily that the artist shall work with things in the round instead of painting their semblances on a flat canvas. Such objects and backgrounds as he can bring to the stage in characteristic form, without suggesting a display of virtuosity, are brought there; such others as cannot be shown in plastic form are indicated by concrete suggestion, and not by pictorial representation. If a church scene is needed, the artist does not paint a picture of a church for a background, but sets up a single pillar or archway, which in its architecture and its arrangement of aspiring lines suggests the calm dignity and heavy solemnity of a church. If a forest scene is called for, the artist no longer paints a canvas with a multitude of trees, each branch and leaf accurately drawn; he is more likely to arrange a series of cloth strips in place of tree trunks, and then light the stage so subtly that the mystery and depth of a forest are atmospherically suggested. If he has a modern room to show, he discards all painted relief, such as moldings, doorframes, mantels, etc., and sim-

Little Theater, not a single painted-perspective scene was used during the season of 1916–17; and I doubt whether a painted drop has been shown in the Chicago Little Theater in all the years of its existence. And these are only signs of a widespread development. Practically every member of the small group of deep-thinking, far-seeing artist-workmen on the American stage has repudiated the painted-perspective theory and method." That all sounds too obvious for words—but it was really revolutionary eight years ago.

plifies lines, masses and furnishings—conventionalizes the room by reducing it to the simplest form in which it will evoke the proper atmosphere. The new stage artist seldom gets away from the use of canvas flats; they are still the lightest and most easily manipulated material for stage building. But he paints no objects *on* the canvas—he paints it instead in flat color. His canvas flat thus appears on the stage as one side of a solid, and not as a picture representing two or more sides in perspective.

When the designer had thus got rid of the artificialities of the old picture setting, he at first accepted a stage barren of any sort of decorative intent. The action is what counts, he said; and he proceeded to strip the stage of everything that might prove an interruption to interest in the action. Simplicity and suggestion were enough. But it was not long before it was noticed that there was a lack somewhere—or an opportunity missed for reënforcing the drama. The realization came that a merely neutral and unobtrusive background did only half its duty to the play.

So, within the limits of the plastic theory and plastic materials, *design* crept in. Painting was taboo, but the old books on pictorial composition were taken down and dusted off. The stage background became decorative in a new way, quietly, in the spirit of the play, saying to the eye what the poetry was saying to the ear. The note of design must be there, whether in the mysterious masses of light and shade created by Craig's manipulation of screens, or in Rollo Peters' colorful romantic scenes for *Josephine* or *The Bonds*

Scene from *Liliom* as produced by the New York Theater Guild. Setting by Lee Simonson. (See pages 193-5.)

of Interest, or in Jones' famous barren post-office room for *The Devil's Garden*. This last, reproduced on page 207 in barest outline, indicates the extraordinary dramatic value that design can bring to a scene: in this case, formality, a place for an examination, an accentuation of the relationship of the characters by the exact placing of the very few pieces of furniture.

Two half-tone plates illustrate plastic design at its best in New York's organizational theaters: Lee Simonson's cottage scene for the Theater Guild's *Liliom*, and Woodman Thompson's setting for the Actors' Theater production of *Malvaloca*.

IV

A sustained decorative treatment as applied throughout a production is what is implied in the word "stylization" as applied to stage setting. But when one speaks the word it is immediately necessary to defend one's position against two sorts of misconception: first that stylization is a ruthless method of transforming a Greek play into a circus performance, or a Shakespearean play into a decorators' picnic; and second, that it provides a method of overwhelming a good play, or redeeming a poor one, by sets that are a show in themselves. This danger of overdoing the setting will always be inherent in the decorative method to a certain extent. But stylization of setting is really nothing more than a method of bringing the scene into harmony with the essential spirit of the play, a unit in reënforcement, a means of beautifying the background to harmonize with the beauty of the poetry and the action. By his own particular style of working, by his individual manner of using line, mass, color, light and shade, the designer may stamp the setting with his own creative genius; but the decorative quality of the setting must be founded on dramatic fitness.

Let me digress to say that despite the general acceptance of the plastic idea, there is a certain type of play in which more latitude may be allowed in the designing—where a certain artificiality and exuberrance of fancy may be carried into the decorative work. In most plays for children, in pure fantasy, in artificial comedy, in any production in which story value, dramatic tension, and tense mood are less important than imaginative turns of thought, surprise and fanciful suggestion, there is possibility of adding to the play's appeal by a compelling symbolism or fantasy in the settings. A classic example is the Moscow Art Theater's mounting of Maeterlinck's *The Blue Bird*, a play which is at least episodic if not definitely undramatic, and so not in danger of having its continuity of meaning obscured by dynamically interesting settings. The Moscow artists tried to visualize the symbolism of the various scenes in their backgrounds, with the result that the action progressed through a series of fairyland pictures of a beautifully imaginative sort. The settings for such productions may legitimately be painted, for here a certain noticeable artificiality is not out of place.

Within the general classification "plastic," perhaps, but quite different from the more or less "real" plastic, there are sorts of stage design that may best be considered under the title "conventions." First of these is the curtain setting. In their search for the antithesis to the painted-picture background, the designer-reformers early fastened upon curtains as an extraordinarily satisfactory, unreal substitute. Black curtains, natural burlap curtains, curtains rich with beautifully wrought embroidery, curtains decorated with posteresque all-over patterns—each had its turn and its place, and occasionally has place to-day. Even when it carried a pictorial design, as in the Barker-Wilkinson *A Midsummer Night's Dream*, the folds belied any realistic intention and disarmed any realism-seeking mind. The curtain in one form or another, indeed, is likely to prove useful to the little and art theaters on occasion for many years to come.

Second convention: screens. Here again there is neutral background, and a plastic medium capable of endless rearrangement and a great range of emotional suggestion. Gordon Craig invented a special type, and I will give considerable space to it in a moment, because of its value to progressive theaters. Corresponding to the embroidered curtains are such formally painted screens as those designed by Lee Simonson for *The Faithful*, and the immense gilded screens that Hermann Rosse has designed for dance-dramas. Of Sam Hume's adaptation of Craig's system, into a permanent outfit of screens and pylons, I shall also write at length a little later. Lee Simonson's "vignette" settings for *The Failures*, illustrated opposite page 164, are in some sense an adaptation of the screen idea, but without any stressing of the anti-realistic intention.

V

It is hardly necessary to treat lighting as a separate topic. I have suggested several times the larger place it assumes in the new stagecraft. It is employed not only as a binding force—as one more means of reinforcing the spiritual mood of the play—but also as a definite means of developing the emotional rhythm. In certain European theaters lighting has all but taken the place of the setting; and in this country the tendency is strongly in that direction.

Just as changes of feeling, thought and emotion can be reflected in the lighting of a production, so can they be suggested in the color arrangement. We are happily rid of the muddy colors of other days, on the stage as in the picture gallery, and a whole new scale of beautiful and expressive shades and tones has been placed at the artist's disposal.

VI

In the search for new methods which will aid in bringing unity to the production, many devices of value to the art theater have been invented. Certain ones are purely mechanical—the revolving stage and wagon stage are examples—and these for the most part are designed to cut down the waits while settings are being changed, thus tending to eliminate from the course of action breaks long enough to have a disillusioning effect. The idea of suggesting an underlying unity of story by letting certain elements of the setting appear in each succeeding scene, has been worked out by diverse methods. Joseph Urban used what he called a permanent skeleton set through all the acts of *The Love of the Three Kings* at the Boston Opera House, and he has staged several other productions with stationary inner prosceniums and portals, achieving all changes in scene by new elements introduced at the back of the stage. Raymond Jonson used a similar arrangement of permanent fore-structure and changing inner scene for some of the productions at the Chicago Little Theater; and Robert Edmond Jones has occasionally used what may be called a half-permanent set in his productions for Arthur Hopkins. He also has set *Love for Love* in a "double" scene that remains throughout the play, in the Provincetown Players' current revival.

But all these devices and machineries and conventions are matters which a brief work like the present one can only touch upon. Every art theater director will have his own theory and will establish his own convention, will determine the degree of his departure from the old realistic staging. Beyond what I have said, I can best refer the reader to Kenneth Macgowan's illuminating and thorough treatise called *The Theater of To-morrow*, and to *Continental Stagecraft* by Macgowan and Robert Edmond Jones. There too can be found a great deal about that further step in radical theories and methods of staging, abandonment of the proscenium-frame picture stage in favor of the architectural stage, the stage which is merely a confessed platform for acting. It is coming, certainly, together with other freeing and expressionistic changes —but again we are on the verge of that argument about representational and presentational types of drama and production, which is beyond the field of this book.

VII

For the little theaters, it is well worth while to take space to describe two systems of simplified and standardized settings that can be used not only with a saving of time and expense, but with increased unity of feeling. None other is quite so suggestive, or quite so valuable to the American art theater in its formative years, as the screen setting, "the thousand scenes in one scene," invented by Gordon Craig.

Craig, arguing from the fact that hundreds of thousands of dollars are wasted annually for scenery that loses all its value when the play's run is over—and this for a type of scenery that is devoid of atmosphere, and usually lacking in artistic value of any sort,—set out to discover a sort of stage scene that would be adaptable for any poetic production. The system of portable folding screens which resulted from his years of experiment solved the problem beautifully, providing atmospheric backgrounds for a surprisingly wide range of play, at exceedingly small cost. But here is a point to be noted: the system is so simple, so devoid of trickery and pretentiousness and extraneous ornament, that only men of deep artistic perception and delicate vision, only imaginative artists and true poets, can obtain the best results from its use. For this reason the invention has not made its way into the commercial theater, and probably never will, despite the immense saving its use would entail. In the Moscow Art Theater's famous production of *Hamlet* all the many and varied changes of a setting were merely rearrangements of a set of Craig's screens. And at the Abbey Theater of the Irish Players the screens were used for poetic plays, with results which mark them as particularly fitted to reënforce the spiritual mood and synthetic impression which are the implied goal of art theater production.

The invention is described in *The Mask*, in an unsigned article but presumably by Gordon Craig, as follows:

"The scene is made up usually of four, six, eight, ten or twelve screens, and, although sometimes of more than twelve, seldom less than four. Each part or leaf of a screen is alike in every particular except breadth, and these parts together form a screen, composed of two, four, six, eight or ten leaves. These leaves fold either way and are monochrome in tint. The height of all these screens is alike.

"These screens are self-supporting and are made either of a wooden frame covered with canvas, or of solid wood.

"With screens of narrow dimensions curved forms are produced, for large rectangular spaces broader leaved screens are used, and for varied and broken forms all sizes are employed. . . .

"Sometimes certain additions may be made to this scene, such as a flight of steps, a window, a bridge, a balcony, and of course the necessary furniture, though great care and reserve must be exercised in making these additions so as to avoid the ridiculous.

"This scene is a living thing. In the hands of an artist it is capable of all varieties of expression, even as a living voice and a living face are capable of every expression. The scene remains always the same, while incessantly changing. . . .

"Through its use we obtain a sense of harmony and a sense of variety at the same time. We may be said to have recovered one of the unities of the Greek drama without losing any of the variety of the Shakespearean drama.

"We pass from one scene to another without a break of any kind, and when the change has come we are not conscious of any disharmony between it and that which has passed."

William Butler Yeats, who had to do with the screens at the Abbey Theater, is quoted in the same issue of *The Mask* as follows:

"The scenery differs entirely from the old style of scenery, and consists chiefly of portable screens, by means of which beautiful decorative effects can be obtained, the working of the screens being based on certain mathematical proportions by which the stage manager can make walls, pillars, etc. . . . a palace almost in a moment, a palace of great cyclopean proportions, and which can be changed again almost in a moment into a room with long corridors, and be changed again into a third and very different scene just as quickly.

"The primary value of Mr. Craig's invention is that it enables one to use light in a more natural and more beautiful way than ever before. We get rid of all the top hamper of the stage—all the hanging ropes and scenes which prevent the free play of light. It is now possible to substitute in the shading of one scene real light and shadow for painted light and shadow. Continually, in the contemporary theater, the painted shadow is out of relation to the direction of the light, and, what is more to the point, one loses the extraordinary beauty of delicate light and shade. This means, however, an abolition of realism, for it makes scene-painting, which is, of course, a matter of painted light and shade, impossible. One enters into a world of decorative effects which give the actor a renewed importance. There is less to compete against him, for there is less detail, though there is more beauty."

After the production of *Hamlet* at Moscow the correspondent of the London *Times* wrote of the screens as follows:

"Mr. Craig has the singular power of carrying the spiritual significance of words and dramatic situations beyond the actor to the scene in which he moves. By the simplest means he is able, in some mysterious way, to evoke almost any sensation of time or space, the scenes even in themselves suggesting variations of human emotions.

"Take, for example, the Queen's chamber in the Castle of Elsinore. Like all the other scenes, it is simply an arrangement of the screens already mentioned. There is nothing which definitely represents a castle, still less the locality or period; and yet no one would hesitate as to its significance—and why? Because it is the spiritual symbol of such a room. A symbol, moreover, whose form is wholly dependent upon the action which it surrounds; every line, every space of light and shadow going directly to heighten and amplify the significance of that action, and becoming thereby something more than its mere setting—a vital and component part no longer separable from the whole."

The last lines are eloquent testimony to the value of this type of setting as an integral part of the production, as a part which, instead of disturbing the action, contributes to the mood. In other words, it is an ideal means to art theater ends, so far as they concern the background of the play.

VIII

Gordon Craig's screens have never been adequately tested in this country. But Sam Hume designed his adaptable setting at the Arts and Crafts Theater on the same theory. He gained inspiration from Craig, and he adopted Craig's principle of an interchangeable scene, and had full knowledge of the mechanical features of the earlier invention. Before describing Hume's setting in detail, I wish to record my admiration for the impressive results he obtained from the eleven variations at the Arts and Crafts Theater during its first season. Putting aside consideration of realistic backgrounds at the Detroit playhouse, and remembering that several of the permanent setting arrangements fell considerably short of the ideal, it is still clear that this was one of the finest groups of stage backgrounds yet devised for a series of plays in an American theater. The point to be remembered, if one is interested in little theater and art theater economics, is this: while gaining superior results artistically, Hume spent for eleven settings not more than the cost of two average settings in other theaters. It is well to remember, too, that the range covered by the eleven scenes included such widely differing requirements as the interior of a mediæval château for *The Intruder*, the Gates of Thalanna for *The Tents of the Arabs*, the wall of Heaven for *The Glittering Gate*, and a Spartan palace for *Helena's Husband*.

The permanent setting included the following units: four pylons, constructed of canvas on wooden frames,

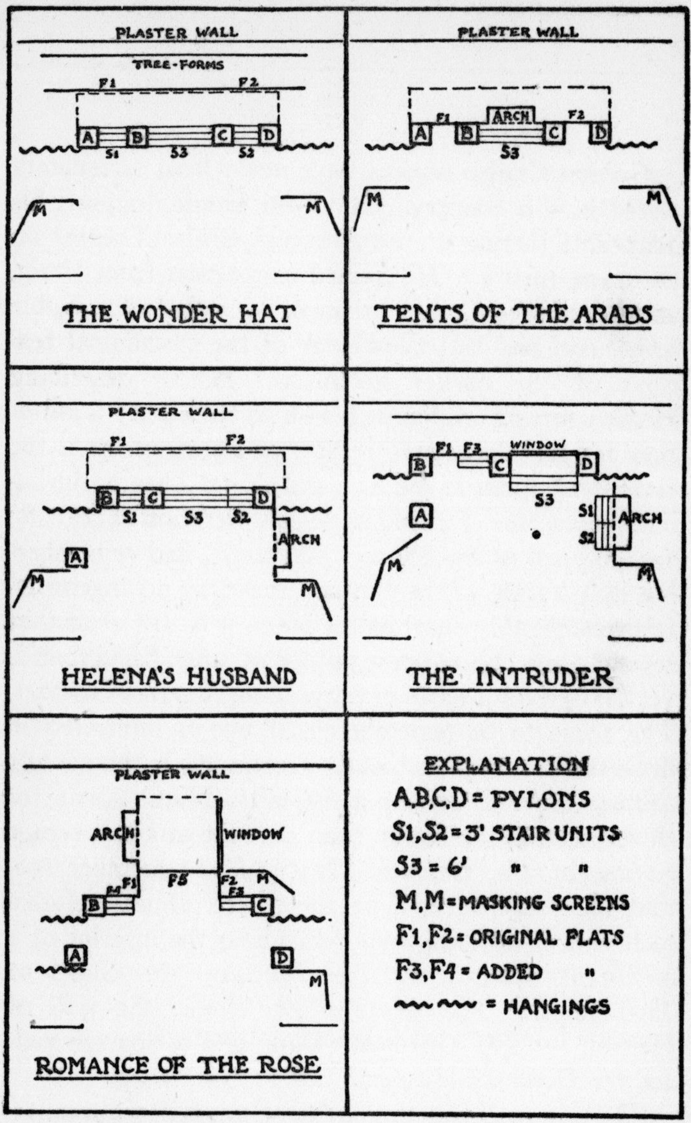

Diagram of five arrangements of the permanent setting at the Arts and Crafts Theater.

each of the three covered faces measuring two and one-half by eighteen feet; two canvas flats, each three by eighteen feet; two sections of stairs three feet long, and one section eight feet long, of uniform eighteen-inch height; three platforms of the same height, respectively six, eight, and twelve feet long; dark green hangings as long as the pylons; two folding screens for masking, covered with the same cloth as that used in the hangings, and as high as the pylons; and two irregular tree-forms in silhouette. An arch and a large window piece were added later.

The pylons, flats, stairs, arch and window were painted in broken color, after the system introduced by Joseph Urban, so that the surfaces would take on any desired color under the proper lighting.

I am reproducing a diagram of five arrangements of the setting. The reader who is sufficiently interested can, by comparing the plans with the halftone photographs of *The Tents of the Arabs* and *The Intruder*, identify the several units and trace the physical changes that resulted in such radical difference in the "looks" of the varying backgrounds. At times the flats were set on their long edges instead of endwise, a fact indicated only by the length of the lines F1–F2 in the diagrams of *The Wonder Hat* and *Helena's Husband*. One of the two flats added toward the end of the season included a door, as seen in the photograph of *The Intruder*.

While the physical changes were as simple as indicated in the diagrams, the atmosphere, under lighting, was so changed with each new variation that it is doubtful whether any but a very few people in the audiences realized that the same elements were reappearing. After the remarkable beauty and appropriateness of the series of settings, the most notable thing about them is their cheapness. Although the original equipment, as seen in *The Wonder Hat*, cost more, perhaps, than the average little theater setting, it was far less expensive than the usual commercially designed set. And the particular point to be noted is that, once installed, changes and additions at very slight cost served to create effects which would have called for an outlay of several hundred dollars for each scene under the usual system. In the ten variations arranged after *The Wonder Hat* the total cost of added pieces averaged less than fifteen dollars for each scene. To the notoriously poor—though often notoriously extravagant—little theaters, such a solution of the scenic problem should be a godsend; although a few brains are essential to the working of the system.

The success of the system as worked out by Sam Hume is dependent upon several factors. First, of course, there is the physical requirement of a stage with a sky-dome or plaster background (a cyclorama drop is a passable substitute), and a flexible lighting equipment. In the second place there must be rigid standardization of the original elements and of each added unit. And most important, let me repeat, there must be a director who combines inventive ability with artistic taste.

The permanent setting at Detroit was used for poetic

Two arrangements of Sam Hume's "permanent setting" at the Arts and Crafts Theater, Detroit. Above, *The Tents of the Arabs;* below, *The Intruder.*

plays, for those productions which demanded atmospheric background rather than definite locality, and occasionally for such a modern interior as that of *Suppressed Desires*. But no attempt was made to extend its function to the mounting of realistic plays; special sets were built for such plays as *Trifles*, *The Last Man In*, and *Lonesomelike*. It happens that the settings for these plays represented one of the weakest spots, artistically, of the whole achievement at the Arts and Crafts Theater; and of course each of these poorer settings cost more than any of the variations of the permanent set. This suggests the possibility of standardizing a modern interior which could be used in variation for practically any modern realistic play. I believe that some experiments have been made in this direction, but without really satisfying outcome as yet.

CHAPTER IX

THE QUESTION OF AUDIENCES AND THE COMMUNITY

THERE are certain likenesses in audiences for the best drama everywhere, and in certain ways the relationship between the creative little theater and its small community corresponds to the relationship between a full-fledged art theater and its New York or Cleveland public. For example, in towns both large and small the audience is likely to be tied to the theater by subscription; and it should be true that any mature or promising institutional theater enjoys the support of important civic organizations. But there are *more* ways in which the audience problems of the little theater and of the mature big-city theater differ; and the major portion of this chapter can be taken as applying to only one group or the other.

I

I have already affirmed my belief that New York would support a dozen art theaters purveying the best old and modern plays as well produced as the Guild's *John Ferguson* and *Jane Clegg* and *Liliom*, or the Actors' Theater's *Hedda Gabler* and *Candida* and *The Wild Duck*. These are productions for which there is always a moderate-sized audience, if the standard of mounting and performance is high enough. There is an intelligent resident audience that prefers this type of play to all others, and there is also a tourist trade in New York from travelers who will seek out the finest the town can offer. But at present it is difficult for any organization to live on this moderate-sized audience alone, because every group playing on Broadway except the Theater Guild is obliged to pay to commercial theater-owners the tribute of high rentals. For a medium-sized theater the lease value is likely to be from seventy-five to ninety thousand dollars a year (or forty per cent of the gross receipts, if the production is booked in by the week). The moment an organization begins to pay that price, it must in self-defense play for its share of the floating audience upon which Broadway managers so largely depend. It must advertise along with the others in the full list of New York dailies, putting a further excess burden of five hundred dollars a week on its offering; it must play the game with the ticket brokers; and it must choose its plays with a broad instead of a special appeal if it is to keep from sinking. In other words, the moderate-sized audience that always exists for really fine offerings is large enough to sustain an economically run company at the fairly small Garrick Theater, somewhat off Broadway, but not large enough to insure success at a full-sized house farther uptown. And any organization that takes the larger house is likely to find itself drawn into the gambling game of production as played by the business-managers, and cocking an eye for the best-seller play. The ultimate solution lies in the fact that an organization can lift the burden of inflated rentals by owning its own building (and subsidy or endowment to the amount of the rental value is all that any group should ever have to ask); and by finding a subscription audience large enough, it can also avoid the artificial burden of large advertising.

In one sense an organization in New York or Chicago or Philadelphia is not likely ever to have a community audience in the intimate sense that a city of fifty thousand inhabitants will have one. The same civic interest does not exist (look at our mayors!), and it is impossible to tie in groups around artistic projects. It will always be more a pay-for-what-we-get sort of audience. But because New York is a metropolis with a reputation as a national art center to maintain, the people of wealth are likely to subsidize anything that looks like a sane step toward a national theater. One wealthy patron gave the Theater Guild financial aid at the moment it most needed a friend; but the Actors' Theater and the Provincetown Players are both sustained at present (if they have losses) by large groups of guarantors. New York, I think, will have two or three real repertory art theaters before London has one.

New York's audience-and-community problem is such a special one, however, that I think the major part of this chapter should concern the audiences of the average or small town.

II

It would be useless to set down a matured art theater, playing the best drama continuously, in the average small city. It would find insufficient audiences to accept its offerings, and it would have no relation to the art life and civic life of its community. It would die for not having its roots in native soil.

Somewhat paradoxically, it seems futile to organize audiences and community theater associations before there are companies aiming to supply the demand for better dramatic fare. Drama League Centers and drama circles of women's clubs have missed half their opportunity by neglecting the creative element in their local theaters. The organizers recognized the deplorable condition of the American stage, and they stirred up people to form audiences and demand better drama; and then, having nothing but an outside knowledge of the theater, they asked the tradition-bound and unenlightened commercial manager to step in and supply some art.

The result is that the country now has an immense audience for written drama, which is a mighty good thing in its way; and this audience is demanding the best in produced drama, but has had little training in recognition and appreciation of what that best will be.

The Drama League Centers, with notable exceptions, have been neglectful of *creative* dramatic enterprises in their own districts. Little theater groups in all parts of the country have complained that they could obtain neither coöperation nor encouragement from the one organization founded ostensibly to aid progress toward better theater art. The Drama League is organized as a league of community art theaters should be, with local self-governing centers loosely joined in a national body. But until it sees the wisdom of locking forces with the creative groups, it will tend to remain primarily a sort of Chautauqua reading circle, and its aid toward a new theater will remain passive. Many of us who have watched its halting progress have felt the more irritated because its opportunity for lasting service is so very great. Under effective leadership and with adequate means it could perform invaluable service as a national clearing-house for the creative producing groups.

The first normal step toward a community theater is likely to be in some such obscure venture as a little theater working on an experimental basis, amateurishly at first, but with intelligent growth toward an ideal. Such practical beginnings, nearly always initiated by a group of enlightened artist-workers, should early receive the support of the enlightened theorists of the community, as represented by such organizations as the Drama League, community arts associations, and colleges. Development should follow in full coöperation. The producing group is the more likely thus to become stabilized with definite relationship to its habitat; and whether looking toward ultimate professionalization or preferring to remain an amateur little theater, it will reach its artistic goal the more quickly and more efficiently for intelligent support.

The audience group must be willing to overlook certain inevitable failures of the producing company at first, not looking for artistic perfection in the beginning. On such foundations will a group of sound community theaters appear in this country. And that will be our national theater.

III

"Community theater" is at best only a relative term. As most of us use the phrase it has nothing to do with the "civic theater" of Percy MacKaye, in which community participation on the stage is the test. His civic theater associations would have nothing to do with the purveying of art for the people, but would only use the art form as a convenient medium for developing a wholesome civic consciousness, through bringing many people shoulder to shoulder in play—which, like an Iowa picnic, is an excellent thing in its way, but has little to do with art enjoyment. "Community theater," moreover, does not necessarily mean a theater which is designed to serve a majority of the people of its city, or even any considerable percentage of the population. If the owning and producing groups have grown up out of native experiment and interest, if the productions reflect the *best* demands of the community in a form acceptable to enough members to keep the institution thoroughly alive, if the price of admission is low enough so that no wide section of the public is excluded through inability to pay for admission, then it is a community theater in a very practical sense.

There is, of course, a wide difference of opinion among little theater directors regarding the relative value of maintaining an art standard and giving opportunity for participation to as many amateur actors as possible. Personally I incline to the view that, in the absence of any considerable amount of intelligent dramatic entertainment on the road, it is incumbent upon the little theaters to supply the best plays right up to the finest standard of production they can attain. In other words I look at it as an artistic and cultural problem rather than as a social problem. If the director cannot build up a more or less permanent company with the best actors he can find—without having to take seriously the plaint that "they don't give Bessie no chance"—he is not likely to be building foundations for a real art theater. I am the less insistent on my own point of view, however, because a critic whose opinion I respect launched a broadside at me after the publication of the first edition of this book, using as text my statement: "Unless we carry the little theaters beyond the ideals most of them stand for, unless we professionalize them while preserving their amateur spirit, unless we organize them efficiently for art production, we shall be little better off than before they came." The answer to this was: "Arbitrarily to compel the little theater to goosestep to some preconceived rhythmic idea is, on the face of it, highly ridiculous. Does not the authentic value and contribution of the small playhouse lie in the concept of insurgency with which it is intrinsically informed?

Does it not consist largely in its ringing note of individuality?" *

Of course no one wants to introduce any goose-stepping hereabouts; it is certain that the wider latitude we have in both artistic and organizational experiment, the better. Every individual idea about the method of stimulating these hundreds of little theaters to their finest contribution should be tried out. Nor can I point to any conclusive evidence that the little theaters with closely organized companies have come any nearer to permanent community service than those with the wide-participation ideal. The great success of the Cleveland Playhouse—almost "professionalized," and so well established that an ideal building is being constructed for it—is offset by the example of the Pasadena Community Playhouse, where "the aim is to use as many different people each year as possible, because this is a community undertaking"—and also successful to the point of having been provided with an extraordinarily fine new home. Among the really little theater groups, I know that the Fireside Players at White Plains, New York, have an understanding that anyone who wants to act shall have a chance to appear before the public in one of the organization's offerings. An interesting fact about this group, by the way, is that it occupies its home jointly with a community church. The building was specifically designed for these two purposes: for church

*Pierre Loving, in the Preface to Frank Shay's *The Plays and Books of the Little Theater*, New York, 1919.

services and for dramatic productions. How far have we traveled, O Christians!

But let me repeat, *personally* I believe the greater contribution to lie with those little theaters which shade their community participation ideal for the sake of building more efficient acting companies.

IV

It is natural that audiences for a really "advanced" art of the theater should not exist in the average American city at present. Because the playhouse became commercialized and its productions stereotyped, theatergoers have been trained in appreciation of the obvious and the sensational, with seldom a chance to form a taste for the phases of dramatic art that are most worth while. Our large audience is unmistakably movie-minded.

But *potential* audiences for the best drama do exist in the average American city. They are unorganized and badly scattered, but can be built up as an art theater grows. I base my opinion here on the experience of Pasadena, Santa Barbara, Berkeley, Dallas, Galesburg, Madison, the State of North Carolina, New Orleans, Toronto, Rose Valley, New York's East Side, Carmel-by-the-Sea, Ypsilanti, Cincinnati, and other points North, South, East and West.

I think that there is not a city of one hundred thousand people in this country where a beginning organization aiming toward an ultimate art theater could not find a supporting audience, granted that the appeal was not too narrow at first, that an expert artist-director was in charge, and that the project was managed in a businesslike way. And this audience would grow with the organization, so that the mature art theater would have its proper community support. Many a smaller town, of five, ten, or twenty-five thousand, is as likely ground for the same seed.

Let me add just one concrete example with figures. The Pasadena Community Playhouse was organized in the usual small way seven years ago. This season it gave twenty-two productions, in 214 performances, to 47,241 people.

V

Most American little theaters lean for their chief support upon a subscription audience. Because they are not endowed, nor capitalized, as is the business theater, they find the security enjoyed under this system necessary to any sort of permanency. But the subscription system has more advantages than the securing of a certain income each season. A subscribing audience always feels a proprietary interest in the theater. It is the link between the producing group and the community. This is a matter of such importance that I think that even an endowed art theater, with its implied economic independence, would be very unwise to abandon the subscription basis. From humble beginnings to maturity it should have its "members."

In Berlin there is a theater, the *Volksbühne*, with more than 100,000 subscribers. It happens in this case that the subscription audience also owns the theater. But the point is that through such organization the producers provide plays better chosen, better acted and better staged than the commercial average, for a charge of twenty-five cents a member (pre-war figures). The saving that makes this revolutionary result possible may be summed up in this way:

No one makes a speculative profit from the theater; there are no failures, and the spectator is not charged, as in the American system, for the play he sees and for two others on which the producer lost money; the actors are employed by the year, and do not have to charge an inflated price for their services, as our American actors do when employed, to make up for long intervals of unemployment; the rental charge is low because the theater does not need to be in the high-rent district, and because it is always in use (American theaters charge against the short season lessee enough to cover the loss accruing during the considerable number of weeks when the building is dark); and there are no traveling expenses, advertising costs are radically reduced, and sundry savings are effected through standardized methods in the producing and business departments.

The chief facts about the *Volksbühne* are worth recording here, for the stimulus they may afford some browsing American theater-organizer. The project is owned coöperatively by an audience that numbers well over 100,000. The members of that audience run their theater just as any other community-owned project must be run, by elected officers. They enjoy the privilege not only of attendance at their own theater's constantly changing productions, at prices that seem ridiculous when compared with our $2.20 to $3.30, but also of attendance at half-a-dozen other leading Berlin theaters, including the State Opera House and the Charlottenberg *Schiller-Theater*, at the same small fees—a privilege made possible because, as an organized audience, they can "buy up the house" at a reduced rate, fill every seat, and distribute the cost pro rata. The organization grew from a small group, that banded together in 1890, chiefly for the purpose of evading censorship, a group called "The Free Folk Stage" and not unconnected with the Socialist movement; this gave way to a "New Free Folk Stage," organized chiefly to secure the directors more power (and also freedom from petty interference by individual members of the audience—coöperation being tempered with a bit of wise autocracy here); then a period of difficulties with both finances and the police led into a period of increasing prosperity which has lasted for twenty years, most of that time with full evening and matinee performances and special performances at other theaters. The constantly enlarging and ambitious society, still mostly workingmen and women, became merely the *Berliner Volksbühne* in 1914, when it built and occupied one of the finest theater structures anywhere.

There is a pretty tale about the financing of the new *Volksbühne* building. First the executive committee put aside a nucleus out of the society's savings. Then members were taxed ten per cent extra on their one-mark entrance tickets, and after a few years, when any member's accumulated taxes amounted to ten marks, he received a card as evidence that he had loaned that amount to the organization. The members thus financed the building by obligatory loans from themselves, loans that bear interest and will ultimately be repaid. They borrowed other capital in a lump sum from the City of Berlin; but it was the members' own loans, paid in two and a half cents at a time, that made the building possible.

The repertory of the *Volksbühne* is one of the most remarkable on record: first for its breadth and catholicity, and second as showing how a *people's* theater repertory may be expected to differ from the usual chosen-from-above, more or less aristocratic play-list of the average endowed theater. It is not surprising that Hauptmann's *The Weavers* should have been one of the great successes of the society's earlier days, or that Ibsen, Shaw, Tolstoy, Gorky and other illuminators of the darker side of the economic shield should be among the most-played authors, or that the revolutionary *Masse-Mensch* should be a recent favorite, turning up regularly once or twice in the weekly schedules of productions. But beyond that there is an interesting reliance on the classics (Shakespeare particularly), on poetic and fantastic plays in general, and on a type of folk-drama that is hardly known in English literature; and there is a notable lack of emphasis on the French type of drama and on the salon sort of comedy.

As to breadth, the *Volksbühne* repertory ranges

The Volksbühne, a people's art theater in Berlin. (Oskar Kaufmann, Architect.)

from the Greeks to Sigurjonsson and von Hofmannsthal, from Shakespeare to the Expressionists Georg Kaiser and Ernst Toller. As evidence of catholicity one might place Goethe beside Wedekind, Maeterlinck beside Schnitzler, Kotzebue beside Shaw and Strindberg. A list of the plays offered to members in the five-year period from 1914 to 1919 (including, I believe, the special productions at other than the home theater) embraced 190 plays, by 115 authors.

Such is the accomplishment of a subscriber-owned theater under wise leadership. (The chief officers and artists concerned are Friedrich Kayssler, general director and one of the leading actors, Jurgen Fehling, regisseur, and Hans Strohbach, stage designer.) It may well serve as reminder to audiences elsewhere.

The subscription system thus not only binds the community to the theater, but when properly managed may prevent so much waste that the productions can be bettered even while the prices are being cut to a fraction of those charged by commercial theaters.

I think that there is not a single forward-looking producing organization, little or big, in America, that does not have its subscribers. One reason why the Actors' Theater, despite some superb productions, finds itself less stable in the New York community than the Theater Guild or the Provincetown Players or the Neighborhood Playhouse, is that its directors have been only half-hearted in their belief in a subscription audience. Each season they have waked up too late to the idea that a large subscription membership is the safest anchor to financial security. The Guild, on the other hand, has made the most of its production record, has wisely pushed ahead to absolute security through the sale of membership tickets. Its subscription list has grown from 150 in 1919 to 600 in 1920, 1300 in 1921, 2800 in 1922, 6000 in 1923, 10,000 in 1924, and 14,000 in 1925. That is a record of popular appreciation, indeed. It also means that today the Guild takes absolutely no risk of financial failure in any production it may desire to give. Its expenses for the season are covered by money in the bank before the first play goes into rehearsal. It is a sort of economic success that assures absolute freedom artistically. Independently of their purchases of membership tickets, the Guild audiences largely financed the building of the new Guild Theater.

VI

The relation of the theater and the community should not be merely that of artist and patron; it should involve a wide influence in shaping the social and recreational life of the city. For the present, it is most important that the little theaters and art theaters do educational work in their communities in an effort to create some sort of public standards of amusement. As the need is so elementary, it is probable that this work can be begun best through the schools and colleges.

At Detroit, Sam Hume counted among his duties as director of the Arts and Crafts Theater the organization and instruction of a class of teachers. These people, he argued, are directing and will continue to direct student productions at the schools, and if they have no other model they will make their staging a poor copy of that seen in the commercial theater. So he set about to teach them the underlying principles of theater production, with special reference to a simplified but genuine stagecraft. In order further to connect the theater's work with the schools a special form of membership was arranged for teachers, and at the later productions the dress rehearsals were opened to invited audiences of students and teachers.

Sam Hume also carried the work of the theater out into the community by lecturing extensively before women's clubs and other organizations; and a wider audience was brought to the theater by lectures delivered by authorities of national and international reputation. Several schools called Mr. Hume into consultation while planning stages for their auditoriums, and this work he regarded as part of his service to the community as director of the theater. To those broad qualities of the artist-director enumerated some chapters back, add ability as lecturer and teacher!

Summer schools devoted to the theory and methods of play production have partly relieved the obligation to teach the teachers. But from New York to Santa Barbara there is a healthful entente between the schools and the progressive theaters.

There is no reason why the art theater should not be a part or even the nucleus of such social centers as many cities are now trying to provide for the use of all their people. The settlement theaters, such as that at Hull House, are embodiments of the idea, but they are a little too closely linked with the redemption of slums to maintain a high artistic standard. We want art theaters in which the best life of the city, and particularly the art life, revolves around the dramatic center.

This idea is more applicable to smaller cities than to such a metropolis as New York or Chicago. The Neighborhood Playhouse in New York, to be sure, fills its niche in one small section of the city, the Jewish East Side, with extraordinary success, and is both socially and artistically of great importance. A real civic theater center for the greater city, however, would have to be on a much larger scale, and it is a question whether a single institution could really be expressive of the community. In many small towns the seeds for such central institutions have already been sown. Frederick Koch is working toward that end in his development of theatrical consciousness in North Carolina. Some of the national foundations fostering the building of community houses have recognized the wisdom of providing for community producing groups, and have tied in dramatic work to the larger center group of activities. In some towns the theater may never climb beyond an amateurish plane; but it will be a vital element in the community life nevertheless. I have in mind at the moment a little theater at Ypsilanti, Michigan. When the first suggestion of such an institution was made, there was little response. But now the Ypsilanti Players have a small playhouse of their own, offering productions at regular intervals, and the organization is perhaps the livest social element in the town. It has provided a bond of interest that unites factions and overrides narrow social distinctions. For eleven successive seasons it has afforded a center both socially and artistically. Many a large city, incidentally, has had less opportunity to see the finest plays of past and present than has this comparatively small town.

How far a theater alone can weave its place into the deeper life of a community was early proved at the Prairie Playhouse at Galesburg, Illinois, where a barroom was remodeled to serve as a playhouse. Here the local center of the Drama League joined hands with the amateur producing group, and the theater became a definite force in the recreational life of the community, a notable social asset, and an institution for the citizens to be proud of. It was unfortunately one of the playhouses later killed by the war, but its lesson is just as important.

Such small-town playhouses are not likely to approach closely the art theater ideal of production. At both Galesburg and Ypsilanti the architectural and mechanical limitations are such that even an inspired artist-director could not hope always to reach the finished standard implied in the term "art theater." While the producers often make a virtue of their necessity, and occasionally secure effects with a fresh loveliness unknown in the commercial theater, they are distinctly limited in achievement of beauty in staging. But even under such limitation there is in their activities a real service to the art of the theater. In the list of Galesburg plays one finds the names of new and unknown authors sandwiched between those of Charles Rann Kennedy, Anton Tchehoff and William Vaughan Moody; and at Ypsilanti the range has been equally wide. In other words, even though the staging may have been cramped, the communities in which such playhouses exist have had tastes of the best in drama; both players and audiences have been influenced toward the best in dramatic literature. When these people visit New York, moreover, they will go to see first, not *Artists and Models* or the *Winter Garden Show*, or *Ladies of the Evening* or *The Bride Retires*, but rather *St. Joan* or *The Wild Duck* or *Processional* or *Cyrano*. In other words, each progressive center, no matter how small or how amateurish, reflects its good work on the activities of all the others.

Following the thought as it applies to a large city, one remembers that the Neighborhood Playhouse and the Provincetown Players and the Guild have had a definite influence on the theatrical business situation in uptown New York. The managers are too shrewd not to watch the crowds going to certain offerings of these outsiders; and while they cannot always capture the qualities that make the organizational productions most worth while, they will modify their offerings a little to meet the competition; and there will be thus a slight advantage to the whole New York community.

In this way the new spirit, finding expression in any

narrow section of a community, reaches out until it affects the whole. Audiences everywhere benefit by its achievement of a new standard of excellence in production—and one more step is taken toward creating a nation-wide audience for the developing art theater.

CHAPTER X

ORGANIZATION AND MANAGEMENT

Henry Irving was fond of saying that "the theater must succeed as a business if it is to succeed as an art." The statement carries a false implication as well as a sound core of truth. It is not true that the theater must pay dividends on the excessive capitalization forced upon it under our abnormal competitive commercial system. It is not even true that a theater must be entirely self-supporting—for we know that art often flourishes under endowment. But whether a theater is economically dependent upon casual audiences or endowed to a greater or less extent, it must be intelligently organized and cleanly administered, or it cannot serve art wholesomely or permanently. The endowed theater must be self-supporting within the terms of its endowment, and every playhouse must adopt common-sense business principles in management, if it is to succeed in creating and perpetuating a worthy art.

Too many little theaters have discounted the value of business efficiency, and there have been innumerable failures on that account. For this reason I wish to emphasize the need for sound management. No little theater, or other organization looking toward art theater production, should initiate activities without a definite placing of control and a predetermined system of administration.

I

Perhaps the plan of organization which has proved most successful is one under which responsibility is three-fold. First, there is a holding group, owning the theater and organization, or representing the owners, which determines the policy and is a court of last appeal for all questions arising in the two administrative departments; second, there is an artist-director who is responsible for every activity behind the curtain, and has complete power in everything pertaining to choice of plays and production; and third, there is a business manager who is responsible for front-of-the-house administration, and who has charge of seat sales, rentals, publicity, bookkeeping, etc.

The controlling group, which must be organized as a self-perpetuating body, necessarily determines the general policy of the theater. If it has not full ownership, it represents the true owners before the world, whether they are merely a larger or smaller group of individuals, or an organized audience, or a municipality. As representative of the community, this holding committee is a go-between responsible to the membership or audience on one side, and holding reins leading to the artist-director and business manager on the other. It must be ready to meet suggestions, demands, and complaints from these three directions. It holds the only check on the director, and it must decide all questions arising between that often-temperamental official and the hard-headed business manager. It must determine such matters as the number of performances to be given, basing its decision on the estimates of producing and business departments; and it must adopt a play policy which will satisfy the audience to a reasonable extent. Needless to say, perhaps, this committee should be composed of forward-looking artists and art lovers, with a safe portion of business sense thrown in by way of balance.

In the case of larger organizations with many interests it may be wise to have an official staff representative of the holding group. In smaller theaters the artist-director stands for the owners or Board, to the public, and in all contacts except those pertaining to business. But when a theater grows to maturity this art director or producing director, who should always be looked to as the head of the organization, is likely to find himself so beset with problems of staging and play finding that he cannot humanly continue the general overseeing of the project. A general administrative officer is then necessary. Thus Theresa Helburn, Executive Director of the Theater Guild, stands to the public as representative of that institution more than any other officer; and Kenneth Macgowan is chief administrative officer of the Provincetown Players, although he enters into the art-life of the organization only coöperatively in the matters of play choice and general planning of productions, and not at all in actual staging of plays. On the other hand, certain artist-directors—notably Sam Hume, Frederic McConnell and Gilmor Brown—have proved themselves combined producing directors and executives, and they have preferred to delegate some stage duties to assistants in order to compass the larger administrative function. Perhaps one should suggest not a rule but a warning: be sure that *some* officer represents the holding group fairly and wisely to all who come with suggestion, complaint or matters that are not strictly routine in either the art or business department.

The ownership of American art theaters, the question whether they will be in the hands of individuals, or of societies more or less responsible to the community, like Art Associations, or of municipalities, is purely a matter of speculation. But it is probably true that private ownership is the method offering fewest advantages, and municipal ownership a goal to which we should work definitely but very, very cautiously.

Private individual ownership is usually destructive of art ideals because the single owner seldom feels any responsibility to the community, and he is interested more in profits than in giving the best drama. If a single owner were inspired by the highest ideals, and through wide experience and breadth of taste could take the place of the controlling group, administering his theater directly through his artist-director and business manager, he might develop a model art theater. But the same limitations pertain here as in the matter of autocratic government. A just and enlightened autocracy is perhaps the best type of government that ever existed; but the benevolent despot is so rare that all the world is driven to seek democracy instead.

Group ownership, ownership vested in a small body of artists, workers and others deeply interested in the theater, has proved successful at the Moscow Art Theater and other institutions in Europe; and it is not an uncommon basis of organization among American little theaters—although most of them do not own buildings, but only the settings, good will and similar assets. Under this system the owners naturally act as the controlling body, as a board administering through the artist-director and business manager. There is nothing in this small-group ownership to prevent the theater from becoming a subscription house, with a definite community relationship, if the owners are sincere in their desire to serve art and their audiences rather than to make speculative profits.

Ownership vested in such a group as trustees for an organized audience, or for the municipality, is an ultimate goal in this country, and a system which has proved phenomenally successful in certain German cities. But it is doubtful whether the ground has been sufficiently prepared for the establishment of a municipal art theater in America. The natural order is to progress from experimental art theater to municipal theater. I have more faith in development of the movement through playhouses owned for the present by groups of artist-workers or by art societies or by trustees for community audiences.

I have very little faith in the development of significant theaters where ownership remains with a group of amateur actors alone. A clear distinction should be made between the old-time dramatic-social clubs and the theaters developed by organizations interested primarily in the art of the theater. The clubs are chiefly interested in the theater production as a social function and as a means of amusing themselves, and ownership of the outfit is unimportant. But when the object of the group becomes rounded-out production, the actor-owner is an embarrassment. The artist-director, being responsible to the actor-owners, simply cannot strike out independently and cast plays to the best advantage artistically. The player-owner is subject to many of the same objections as the actor-manager of the commercial theater. The system presents so many dangers that it would be wise for any amateur dramatic club desiring to rise to the little theater or art theater level to appoint a controlling board including a majority of non-actors, and then submit entirely to the decisions of that board.

One other sort of association ownership merits attention. When two long-established art associations opened new buildings in the autumn of 1916, each containing a complete theater equipped according to progressive standards, it seemed to some of us that a new and significant phase of theater progress in this country was being recorded. An outcast among the arts was being restored to a dignified place beside painting and sculpture: the idealists and recognized artists of two communities were coming into direct touch with theater production. As a matter of fact both of those art organizations long ago gave up theatrical producing on their own accounts, making their stages available to outside little theater groups but withdrawing from active participation. The St. Louis Artists' Guild had a brief but creditable history dramatically. The Arts and Crafts Theater in Detroit lasted long enough to complete one of the most interesting and instructive experiments in the larger history of the insurgent movement. In the last analysis I think that the Arts and Crafts Society killed off its dramatic department because its theater was too successful. The organization had existed for many years as one of the livest arts and crafts associations in the country. When its new building was completed in 1916 the theater was included as an experiment in accordance with the wishes of a few interested officers and members, and under the contagious enthusiasm of the visiting Sam Hume. Even then there were objectors. And when the theater suddenly blossomed into the most active and most popular department of the Society, there was bound to be agitation to prevent its further overshadowing the original activities of the group behind it. In its very success, the theater carried reasons for its destruction. There were other contributive causes, of course. But there can be no doubt that there are art organizations which will find such a spectacular art as theater production so dwarfing that it should be approached with caution and great forethought.

At the moment of writing, the Chicago Art Institute is completing the Kenneth Sawyer Goodman Memorial Theater, a model full-sized building for repertory production and experimental work. A special dramatic department of the Institute has been organized, under the direction of Thomas Wood Stevens. The other

The new Santa Barbara Community Theater (Lobero Theater). The attractive green room, shown in the lower photograph, is indicative of the restored dignity and standing of the actor under the art theater form of organization. (George Washington Smith, Architect.)

outstanding example of a theater fostered by an art association is the Santa Barbara Community Playhouse, administered under the larger Santa Barbara Community Arts Association. It too has a beautiful new building, with a full-sized auditorium and a stage especially designed for experiment and the newest methods of production. In this case, of course, the theater unit is nearer a separate entity, and there is no cause for uneasiness over its competition with the other art interests of the larger organization.

Personally I believe that there is an immense benefit to be gained by the progressive theaters through close coöperation with the well established art societies; and it is not at all unlikely that many an American art theater of the future will be founded and developed through the activities of such organizations. They offer those advantages of a definite foothold in the community, permanency of organization, and partial endowment (since they usually own their buildings), which are so important in the formative period of a theater's career. I may add incidentally that, if the experience at Detroit was a fair example, the dramatic activity will in turn bring certain benefits to the art society—the new vitality which comes with awakened interest in a new art, and wider community interest through the bringing of a new audience to the society's building.

II

Of the second of the departments existing under the three-unit system of organization, the producing department, much has been written in earlier chapters. Of the duties and powers of the responsible head, the artist-director, I have already said enough. But I wish to emphasize one point: the artist-director must have *complete* charge of every activity connected with staging. To him, and to him alone, the electrician, the scene designer and builder, the costumer and the actor must look for their orders. His one limitation must be that of the size of his budget. Beyond that he should be free from interference by the business manager or by the controlling group above. That group may remove him if a production has in their estimation failed. But while the production is in preparation they must maintain a "hands-off" policy.

It has been because of the failure to observe this clear division of power, this even balance of authority and responsibility, that many a company has broken up in confusion. Failure to establish a definite line between the controlling group and the producing group, and failure to give the artist-producer a free rein, wrecked the important Los Angeles Little Theater, although some notable productions were given in 1916–17, and the theater gave a start to one of the foremost stage designers in the country, Norman-Bel Geddes.

The placing of complete control of the stage in an artist-director's hands does not mean that coöperation of artists in staging is impossible. On the contrary, there will usually be the fullest coöperation of the director with the members of the controlling committee and other artists directly interested in the work. The point is that the director should be left free to take the first step toward such coöperation; it should not be forced upon him. He may even want a costume committee or a staging committee, but he should not be put under any obligation to work with a group or person. A little tact on his part may help, however!

It is noticeable that the most important little theaters in the country are those in which the directors have had broadest powers and greatest freedom from interference.

III

In taking up the duties of the business manager, I must make clear at the start that I am talking about the problem of the *little* theaters only. The business manager of an organization like the Theater Guild or the Actors' Theater, where there is direct competition with the speculative "big" theater, must be a man with a specialized knowledge of the game as it is played on Broadway: he must be conversant with all the tricky clauses of leases, sharing contracts, route sheets, agents' advice-sheets, authors' contracts, etc., in addition to knowing the routine of box office management, accounting, publicity and house management. It is a field entered by so few of the insurgent theaters, however, that I do not feel that space should be given to details here. When a developing art theater comes to the place where Broadway problems are to be met, it is necessary to find the man who knows both types of theater. A great deal of information about the running of a Broadway show is collected in Arthur Edwin Krows' admirably complete book *Play Production in America.* With so little of professional business advice, I turn to the other sort of playhouse.

The business manager is too much of a rarity in the American little theater. Whereas the artist was entirely displaced by the businessman in the commercial theater, the businessman has too often been lost in the visionary artist in the amateur theater. It was natural that the revolt should be carried to extremes, and that institutions without centralized responsibility and with volunteer administration should neglect, if not scorn, business efficiency. People usually join such organizations because they are interested in art, and they avoid the thankless tasks of selling tickets, keeping books, and house management. But little theaters have made their most serious mistake in this direction. They would gain if they would realize that "noncommercial" does not necessarily mean—indeed, must not mean—unbusinesslike. If they cannot find a volunteer worker to carry on the hard work of the business department, they will save in the end by employing a manager. Indeed, to initiate little theater or art theater work without a capable man in charge of the business department is to court failure.

In a sense the business manager is just as important as the artist-director. At any rate a failure in his department is quite as certain to wreck the whole enterprise. He should be as deeply interested in the theater, and he should be ready to make the same sacrifices of time and effort for it. He must have as complete charge before the curtain as the artist-director has behind. His relation to the holding group is that of the supervising manager of a business corporation to his board of directors. His relation to the artist-director is limited to a determination of the amount to be expended by the producing department. Having determined the probable income for the season, he is able to say to the artist-director (through the controlling board): "You may spend so much on the entire series of plays, which means approximately such-and-such an amount for each production." As to the relative expenditure on different items, for costuming, for instance, or lighting, or settings, he properly has no authority, so long as the director keeps within the gross amount of his appropriation. As to possible friction between the business manager and art director, there is always a way of settlement through the board to which both are responsible. And let me add that it is better to have such friction if the questions involved will not otherwise be brought up. Dodging the issue of control over expenditures has wrecked more than one theater. I know of one little theater that inadvertently spent two thousand dollars on its first production, and right then and there killed the whole project—because no business manager held a check on what was being paid out by the producing department.

The duties of the business manager of the little theater fall naturally into four divisions: ticket sales, including subscriptions and box office sales; house management; advertising; and the duties of a treasurer, bookkeeping, paying out moneys, and budget-making. Of the first two of these divisions little need be said. The types of subscription, whether or not there shall be a subscription committee for a personal canvass of the community, and arrangements for ticket sales to the public, are matters that have to be determined by special conditions. Under house management are grouped such duties as organizing a force of ushers, attending to auditorium and lobby lights, ticket-taking, janitor service, and, if the organization owns its theater, rentals. These are matters which will be taken care of by common sense—if a sensible manager is definitely charged with them in the first place.

IV

The work of the business manager in his capacity as treasurer of the theater should be as thoroughly systematized as that of any corporation. Not only to safeguard against conscious or unconscious dishonesty, but also in order to make possible accurate estimating of the theater's current status and future possibilities, it is necessary to keep strict account of every penny paid in or disbursed. No materials should be bought, or bills paid, without receipts being obtained. Only thus can the bookkeeper be assured of absolute accuracy. This lesson was learned by experience at the Arts and Crafts Theater. At the first production of the series, purchases of stage accessories and incidentals were made at random. When accounts were made up not only was there a question of exactly what the total cost had been, but it was impossible to make out an itemized list of expenditures, thus preventing accurate budget-making for the future. It was necessary to make a general expense charge which prevented exact apportionment of charges against the varied departments at the end of the year. This lesson once learned, a system was adopted which made necessary a written record of every expenditure. When an expert accountant reported his examination of the books to the subscribers at the end of the season, he pointed out that this theater, in contrast to many others in the non-commercial class, not only finished the season with a surplus, but knew exactly where every cent of its five thousand and odd dollars had gone, with the exception of the general expense item from the first play. This sort of common-sense administration means increased confidence among the theater's supporters, firm foundations for every new project, and peace of mind for director, manager, and owners.

The bookkeeping system adopted at the Arts and Crafts Theater was of the ordinary double-entry sort. By taking a trial balance at any time it was possible to know not only the standing of the theater as a whole, but whether the production in hand was keeping within estimates. A balance was taken after every production, and it was then possible to readjust apportionments for the remainder of the season.

One cannot emphasize too strongly the importance of planning ahead and seeing the necessary money in sight before launching a series of productions. Budget-making is, indeed, the first important step after preliminary organization has been effected. Of budgeting at the Moscow Art Theater, Oliver Sayler writes as follows, in *The Russian Theater under the Revolution:*

"The Art Theater is an institution. It has its own home, its own company, its own clientele, its own faithfully built past, its own carefully analyzed future. Each year it has a budget which faces facts as relentlessly as a budget of a bank or an insurance corporation."

Every little theater group should sit down to plan a season with just that "relentless" facing of facts.

Usually the director and controlling board make a rough estimate of the probable cost for the season. Then the manager and subscription committee start their campaign. After the field for subscriptions has been canvassed so that a fairly accurate estimate of the income can be made, the director will probably have to make revised cost estimates. But the final budget (because the only one based on the amount of money actually available) will be that made at the time actual work on the first production is begun.

I wish to emphasize also the wisdom of economizing on the first production of a season. The tendency to "splurge" at the beginning is one of the most prevalent and serious evils in the little theater field. More than one worker has told me that a safe system is to deduct ten per cent of the subscription money for overhead expense and permanent equipment, and then divide the balance by the number of productions, in order to find the amount to be spent on the first production. In other words, do not count at all on box office sales, but make your beginning performance on the basis of subscription returns only. Doubtless there will be some sales to the general public, but at the start no one ever knows just how small they may be. Usually they turn out to be about one-third of the most conservative estimates. After the first production is over, it is possible to revise estimates to include money taken in at the box office, and to plan more expensive productions on that safe basis.

If the theater does not own its home, the rent charge must be added to the ten per cent allowed for overhead expense and permanent investment; and at the beginning of a theater's career there will be extra expense for initial equipment. Other items will also have to be accounted for in apportioning the income under special conditions. But the point to be remembered is that the business manager must always be in a position to say to the Board, "Your next production cannot safely cost more than such-and-such an amount." And the artist-director must trim his budget to come within that amount. If he complains that he is hampered by the low expenditure allowed, the controlling group can point out only two ways to meet the situation: choose plays less expensive to produce, or cut down the number of productions. For the first law of little theater economics is that the cost of production must be kept within the means available.

V

In setting down here lists of the expenditures and receipts of a typical American little theater, I do not mean to suggest that these can be made the basis of a budget for a mature art theater scheme. Beyond pointing out that sound business management is necessary to the ideal institution, as it is to its forerunner, the little theater, one can say little definitely about the administration of a true repertory art theater. There is no experience on which to base estimates. It is necessary to learn by establishing such theaters and applying common sense during the first year—or by working forward phase by phase from the present amateur basis to the professionalized-amateur basis.

But the following record should prove valuable to beginning groups, and suggestive to other theater workers in the amateur field. The Arts and Crafts Theater represented a typical phase through which the *pre*-art theater must pass.

In studying these figures one must take into consideration certain variable quantities and make allowance for items which differ as one moves from city to city. First it is to be remembered that the Society of Arts and Crafts owns its building, and therefore the item of rent does not appear. The settings were for the most part constructed in the theater, and so cost considerably less than those bought from scenic studios; and there was also a large saving through the frequent use of variations of the existent permanent setting, and through volunteer labor in painting other settings.

With those reservations the figures are typical. (I am not changing the figures in this new edition, even though some items, such as lumber and hardware, would be higher. Little theater directors tell me that the total is not far from the present average.)

EXPENDITURES FOR SEASON OF FIVE PRODUCTIONS

First production	$ 990.35
Second production	954.24
Third production	925.90
Fourth production	866.99
Fifth production	1,099.13
Overhead expense (organization, box office, etc.) *	519.24
Permanent properties	50.82
Total	$5,406.67

APPORTIONMENT OF EXPENDITURES

Royalties			$ 315.00
Properties			143.75
Costumes			519.91
Settings:	Lumber	$142.65	
	Dry goods	61.24	
	Paints	56.23	
	Hardware	130.98	
	Labor	126.00	517.10
Electrical supplies and electrician			100.49
Extra labor (carpenter and electrician)			102.75
Stage-hands			95.25
Wigs and make-up			83.00
Music			39.00
Printing			273.85
Typing parts			15.95

* This overhead charge does not, of course, include the director's salary. One month's salary is charged against each of the five productions.

Cartage	35.09
Director's salary (five months)	2,500.00
General expense *	665.53
Total	$5,406.67

RECEIPTS

Subscriptions	$4,412.50
Box office sales	1,083.75
Total	$5,496.25

The box office sales were as follows: 1st production, $214.75; 2nd production, $130.00; 3rd production, $215.50; 4th production, $238.50; 5th production, $285.00. There was thus a steady gain in sales from the second play to the last.

For a large class of little theaters the average expenditure will be nearer five hundred dollars a production than the eleven hundred indicated here. At the other extreme, for an art theater operating in New York, the annual turnover is likely to be close to half a million. The Actors' Theater, I think, had a gross average annual expenditure of about four hundred thousand dollars during its first three seasons. The Theater Guild, on the basis of its fourteen thousand subscribers, starts with over two hundred thousand dollars in its treasury for the coming season's work, with box office sales from its three theaters not touched. It had a gross turnover well over a million

* This item includes box office expense, advertising, fees to lecturers, and the unapportioned item mentioned on page 241, as well as the usual incidentals.

dollars this season. But these figures perhaps should be concealed from little theater directors!

VI

Advertising is a matter of puzzlement to the average little theater group. The mature art theater, playing continuously, will have to announce its offerings through newspaper columns; but ultimately even it will save much that the commercial manager now spends for display space in the papers and on billboards. And for the average little theater it is a question whether any sort of bought advertising pays. Those of us who had to do with the project at Detroit, at any rate, became convinced that publicity for such a theater depended on pleasing the audiences so that they talked about the productions and encouraged other people to come. The only productions advertised in the newspapers were the second and third in the series; the box office returns on the second were the lowest during the season, and the gain shown on the third was not such as would indicate that the advertising had any effect on attendance. The money paid to the newspapers seemed to have been dead waste.

The publicity gained through newspaper criticisms likewise seemed to have little effect on the growth of the theater. At first an effort was made to interest the dramatic critics. The leading morning paper boasted that its dramatic department was directed by the dean of American critics. This writer not only refused to cover the first production at the Arts and

Crafts Theater, but did not once set foot in the house during the season. He wrote amiably enough of musical comedies and other importations from Broadway, but he let it be known that it would be beneath his dignity to attend the productions of unpaid actors. The critics of the evening papers proved to be less case-hardened, and even though the assignment was given as often as not to a sporting writer or a cub reporter, the reviews toward the end of the season showed many gleams of intelligent appreciation and criticism.

Detroit, unfortunately, is not an exceptional city in the matter of dramatic criticism. Enlightened and unprejudiced reviews are far too rare. It was part of the theatrical trust's work to stifle honest criticism, and to gain control of all channels of publicity. American newspaper owners bowed to the system as a rule. That was nearly thirty years ago; but even to-day the relation between many a paper's advertising department and its dramatic reviews is such as to make newspaper honesty a matter for serious speculation.

The venal press, to my mind, has had much to do with the degradation of the theater in this country, and particularly with the apathy with which the public has come to view the playhouse. At first the papers destroyed all dramatic standards by printing what they were paid to print, regardless of the value of the play in question. But the public was not long fooled. Intelligent people merely realized that they could not believe what they read in the papers, and stopped going to the theaters unless they read in some reliable magazine review that a certain play was worth while. It is this attitude which now makes the way of the progressive theater difficult, and which largely nullifies the great aid the newspapers might otherwise extend to the little theaters. We need a new standard of criticism as well as a new theater.

In New York the standard of critical intelligence is a little higher, perhaps. One could name half a dozen newspaper and magazine critics who combine honesty with the ability to judge and write. There are far too many reviewers, however, with an irresistible show-off complex. A facility for clever writing betrays them. Beyond that, they are prone to judge every offering in relation to the taste of sophisticated Broadway.

VII

Endowment or subsidy is probably necessary to the development of the best type of art theater. In insisting upon good business management I have tried clearly to make the reservation that this does not necessarily mean complete self-support. Business efficiency means merely elimination of waste, and when one has it, one may still need to lean upon a subsidy. It is certain that a theater searching for the highest ideal must have aid in the beginning; and even in its maturity an endowment is likely to make it a real art institution instead of a compromise.

In Europe the best theaters are seldom expected to succeed as speculative business ventures. The most important theaters in France and Germany, with a few exceptions, are to be found in the list of those receiving state, municipal, or private subsidies. When one thinks of the playhouses in which greatest progress has been made toward the new synthetic ideal of production, one remembers that the Moscow Art Theater, now a profitable affair, was able to get through its early years only by the generosity of a wealthy amateur; and the Irish Players survived their early struggles by grace of Miss Horniman's subsidy. In this country the Neighborhood Playhouse, the Theater Guild, the Provincetown Players, the Actors' Theater, the Santa Barbara Community Theater, and most of the other significant projects have enjoyed financial support continuously or at some crisis in their careers. In some cases this aid amounts to permanent freedom from the rent burden. But there is not one real endowed art theater in the country.

When a writer or an artist says that he wants endowed theaters, people begin to talk about the New Theater, or others made in its image. I have already pointed out that that institution was not really endowed; and even if it had been, it would have had to go through many radical changes to become a true art theater. We do not want institutions of that sort, and we especially do not want theaters similarly unrelated to their communities. What I wish to see is wise subsidizing of the really progressive little or art theaters that have their roots in native soil, with a growing endowment as they progress toward art theater stature.

No sort of endowment is worth while if it gives an

unenlightened or unsympathetic rich man control over productions. The stage must be left to the artists, without interference from those who have made their activity possible. It is unwise, moreover, to give patrons a reward in the shape of an option on the best seats in the house. Endowment should be absolute, leaving the theater free economically and artistically. It should provide for administration through a controlling board, which should be representative of the community and which should have artistic insight enough to employ the right artists. Beyond that provision the rich man should make no restrictions on his gift.

It seems to be the rule in Anglo-Saxon countries that art must thrive on starvation or die. Our commercial organization often makes no provision for adequate return to the artist for his product. The more unusual the quality of the art, the less is offered in exchange for it. Those who have the means to encourage the creative artist have too often lacked the taste and discernment necessary to recognize the worthy, and the passion for art which would make their giving seem necessary. Achievement of the ideal art theater, nevertheless, largely depends upon opportunity created by moneyed people. Personally I sometimes wonder how those with the money-power of the community can so easily fail to see the true and ultimate value of things—can so entirely overlook the chance to do a *lasting* service (and incidentally achieve a lasting fame) in the building of civilization. For I believe passionately in art as a force for salvation—

that the things art brings, beauty and spiritual growth, are the most important things in human life. Perhaps when the little theaters and art theaters show that they have declared for sound business management, as well as for art, we shall have a chain of wisely endowed efficient art theaters from the Atlantic Coast to the Pacific.

CHAPTER XI

BUILDINGS AND EQUIPMENT

WHEN artists of the theater set out to capture that elusive thing called mood, they proceed by bringing harmony into every related part of the production. In voice, in movement, in lighting, in scene, they attempt to create an atmosphere which will be all-pervasive, and which will project itself as a spiritual spell over the spectators in the auditorium. But they are handicapped at the start if the building in which the play is presented does not serve to foster that mood, if it tends to destroy rather than reinforce the spiritual *milieu* of the production. The synthetic ideal has a very definite connotation in relation to theater architecture; the connection is such, indeed, that one cannot insist too strongly upon the necessity of housing an art theater in a noble building.

I

American theater architecture until very recently tended to pretentious, ornate, and vulgar imitations of showy French models. When architects approached the problem of building a playhouse they accepted a totally false conception of their duty. They saw the theater as a place of amusement designed to attract the money-spending public, and so they reflected its commercial character in glitter, gaudiness and red-plush pretentiousness. They accepted the businessman's estimate of the theater as the home of "the show business." And so their buildings ranged from a type neighboring on the sensational ten-cent moving-picture house to a type conceived as a sort of Coney Island for intellectuals. They found what they considered authoritative precedent for "heaping it on" in that culmination of the French-Italian social-dramatic ideal, the ornate Paris Opera House.

During the last dozen years, however, a number of less showy houses have been built on Broadway and at scattered places throughout the country. For the most part these recent theater buildings are comfortable for the greater part of the audience, and quite often the useless aristocratic boxes have been omitted, and the stages have been designed with fairly adequate facilities. They suffer, however, from being built not from any distinctive point of view, but with a wholesale eye to any sort of audience that may come to any sort of commercial show that the building may house for a few weeks.

And so to-day the average American theater is out of key with many things that the new art of the theater stands for. It is neither simple nor beautiful; it not only fails to reinforce actively the mood evoked by the play, but it often is not even neutral and reposeful enough to leave the spectator's mind free to enjoy that mood. A majority of the existing playhouses in America must be abandoned by the insurgents to the commercial theater, together with most of the people and plays in them.

II

Of the examples of wholly satisfying theaters in this country, one can go back to the Little Theater and the Neighborhood Playhouse in New York as perhaps the earliest. It is there also that the Theater Guild has just completed its new home, a building structurally and materially very fine, although curiously an imitative reversion to a period style in its decorative features. It begins at the right point, with a perfectly spaced stage and an auditorium properly related to that; and its plant as an institutional theater is complete: offices, school, rehearsal halls, green room, subscribers' club room, etc.

Three recently built theaters in California come nearer to the ideal in carrying the "feel" of an art theater into the decorative elements. They were designed with a sense of the craftsmanship of building, and with an eye not on New York or Paris or on books about period architecture, but with local conditions and native materials and traditions in mind. The buildings speak the same devotion that is the driving force of the producing groups occupying them. The Pasadena Community Playhouse, besides thus fulfilling the more idealistic functions, is materially as complete as any institutional playhouse in the country, with one of the most modern stages anywhere, an auditorium seating eight hundred, a green room many times the size of the Guild's, wardrobe room, sewing room, ample offices and directors' room, a recital hall with stage (which can be utilized for rehearsals and experimental productions), and several shops. The Santa Barbara Community Theater (Lobero Theater) is likewise fitted perfectly to its use, both materially and atmospherically. It seats a smaller audience, 630, but its stage is generously large, 35 by 74 feet with 72 feet height, and it is even more complete in its facilities for building and storing its own settings.

The third example, the Theater of the Golden Bough at Carmel-by-the-Sea, is smaller and has a type of stage designed for one special theory of production. But it is no less beautiful a building in its simplicity and appropriateness, and no less a result of a distinctive vision of the art of the theater.

That perhaps is the most significant point about all three buildings: they reflect in their design and decoration the underlying principles of the art of the theater. In their outward aspects they are marked by those things which distinguish the new movement from the old tendencies. They are characterized by simplicity, sincerity, reticence and reposefulness. They are pleasing in an unobtrusive way, and not in the boastful manner of the Paris Opera. They harmonize with some other phase of dramatic art than its surface glitter.

Other buildings with somewhat the same distinctive modern-theater quality are either under construction or planned for progressive groups. The Goodman Theater of the Art Institute at Chicago promises to be beautiful and quite different from any existing playhouse. The theater being put up by Yale University

The Theater of the Golden Bough at Carmel-by-the-Sea, California. An experimental art theater, built by Edward G. Custer, wherein local tradition rather than New York or Parisian models determined the architectural features.

for Professor George Pierce Baker under the Harkness gift should be close to a model for experimental groups. The Cleveland Playhouse, if present plans carry, will have the first building including both a complete community theater and a complete experimental theater annex.

When I write that the decorative features of a theater should be characterized by simplicity and sobriety, rather than gorgeousness, I am even less concerned about the façade than I am about the interior of the auditorium. Restfulness there is doubly a desideratum. There should be absolute exclusion of distracting ornament and unmeaning detail. For it is concentration that one wants to induce. One does not imply exclusion of either richness or color in so saying, for a subdued richness is perhaps the exact atmosphere for an attentive audience, and there are colors that are reposeful and conducive to a contemplative mood.

Is it necessary to add that the art theater will be democratic? That it will offer a complete and satisfying view of the stage from every seat? That the old horse-shoe style of auditorium will give way to the simpler form adopted by Littmann and others of the leading progressives? That the chairs will not be deeply cushioned in one portion of the house, decently covered in another, and merely bare wooden benches in another? And of course I cast my vote against having any boxes in a sensible theater. They are relics of a barbaric era, when the display of wealth was a primary aim, and when the social occasion was more important than the dramatic.

III

The architect who plans an art theater must be trained in more than the æsthetic requirements of art theater production; he must have wide knowledge of the technical demands as well. He must be a very close student of modern stagecraft, or his building may prove to be out-of-date and impossible for the new artist of the theater when the first production goes on. He must know that a plaster dome (or provision for a very special sort of cyclorama) is an absolute necessity. If the owners are ready to pay for all that the artist asks, the architect must be informed about revolving stages and sliding stages. He must know also what the artist means by "fixed portals" and "inner proscenium," and he should know what has been done toward the invention of a satisfactory adjustable proscenium. He must know why Fortuny set out to revolutionize stage lighting, what he accomplished, and what modifications later artists have made by way of improving his system. In this matter of lighting equipment particularly the architect must have the most comprehensive knowledge, if he would do justice to the producers who will use his theater. For it is no longer possible to let out to an electrical firm a blanket contract for "a lighting system."

As a matter of fact there is hardly an architect in the country to-day who combines the necessary knowledge of his own art and of the intricate fire and safety laws with the necessary experience on a stage. For the reform in stagecraft has been developing so rapidly that only those working continually in the progressive theaters know absolutely which of the new inventions are practical and which are more dangerous than useful. The really important architect cannot take time to experiment day in and day out with the latest innovations; and as yet there are no books that tell one-tenth the story.

For a group planning to build a little theater or a big theater—indeed, any building at all approaching art theater standards—I should advise just one solution of the stage equipment problem: call in one of the really progressive artist-directors, and let him and the architect fight it out, with the provision that the artist-director's word shall be final in all questions of equipment behind the curtain.

Do not let the architect do it alone—we have more than enough monuments to his ignorance—and do not let him work it out with the sort of professional advice he is likely to call to his aid from the business theater. Call in, rather, an experienced artist of the type of Sam Hume or Maurice Browne or Lee Simonson or Norman-Bel Geddes or Irving Pichel. These people know the stage and stage equipment in the light of the new ideals. Their advice is likely to save the theater from the necessity of making expensive alterations later—and it will save a deal of cussing and disappointment on the part of the artists.

I think that the architects of the theaters described above were in consultation with the foremost art theater "decorators" and directors in this country; and most of the groups had sent observers to Europe—

in this case meaning Germany—to see the finest theaters there. It is certain that no designer of a playhouse knows the architectural background of the new movement unless he has studied the work of Max Littmann, the Munich architect who revolutionized the form of the European auditoriums. For a later phase he should know the work of Oskar Kaufmann, who has brought a more radical modernism into the decorative features. But the time is fast coming when by making the rounds of American art theater buildings—New York, Chicago, Pasadena, Santa Barbara, Carmel, Cleveland—he can reach a pretty fair estimate of the value of various types of equipment and design in the working out of his special problem. There will be something wholesome, too, about our Eastern architects turning their faces West to learn about appropriate American design.

IV

The size of an ideal art theater is a matter for speculation rather than for estimate on the basis of experience. The very large theater is doubtless passing. The house seating two thousand or more people is going out of fashion because its dimensions are such that the intimacy now demanded is impossible there. On the other hand, there is a tendency on the part of the insurgents to make their auditoriums too small, even where space and expense do not dictate a limit. Littleness is made a fetish, and many a group will waken later to the fact that the size of its auditorium is limiting its artistic development.

My own ideal theater would provide a seating capacity of seven or eight hundred. It is by no means certain that a repertory playhouse of that size could be made a financial success in an average American city without a substantial subsidy. But it seems to me that such a theater would come nearest to combining economic independence with a satisfying intimacy of atmosphere. It might be possible to bring the number of seats up to approximately one thousand and still avoid the barn-like atmosphere of most of our existing theaters.

In other words, a theater seating fewer than seven hundred people is likely to demand, for continuous art theater production by a paid company, a larger subsidy than any we can now reasonably expect; and a smaller theater, moreover, will not be able to serve its city as a community playhouse in any wide sense. On the other hand, a theater seating more than a thousand is likely to be too vast in proportions to foster the sense of intimacy and to keep the attention of all the spectators concentrated on the stage. The ideal art theater figure seems to lie between these limits.

V

I have said nothing about planning dressing-rooms. I take it for granted that the architect will consider that the art theater is to be used by ladies and gentlemen, and that their dressing-rooms are to be quite different from the pens provided in too many commercial theaters. He will remember, too, that the green room disappeared from the American playhouse only when businessmen got the upper hand, and he will restore it in his design. And if he can make space available by any sort of manipulation, he should add a rehearsal hall.

But now that I am writing about what he *might* do, instead of what he *must* do, let me add that the theater I dream of—the building I shall have when I am considerably older and immeasurably wealthier than now—will be a double theater. It will have a large auditorium and a small one—one for the usual types of drama, and the other for very intimate plays and for experiments. And both these auditoriums will be beautiful according to the principles I have tried to suggest at the beginning of this chapter—only they will be a little more reflective of radical architectural thought than I have advised for other folks. Both stages will be equipped under the supervision of the most enlightened artist-director in the country. And there will be a library for study as well as a rehearsal hall. And if I am very wealthy indeed, there will be an open-air theater by way of annex.

Yes, it is only a dream. But only when a number of us dream such things shall we be able to jolt the architect out of his preoccupation with theater ideals and theater forms of an age that is as dead as Bulwer-Lytton and Boucicault. Only as we dream of the ideal shall we have something as finely satisfying as the half dozen existing exceptions to the popular rule—the rule of making the playhouse a gilded barn of commerce.

CHAPTER XII

UNREALIZED IDEALS

THIS book has been largely about unrealized ideals, and the title of this epilogue might stand over more than half the chapters. The artists in the theater stand only on the threshold of achievement, and the art theater of the future looms up as a growing half-imagined thing. But I wish here at the end of my book to stand facing forward at that threshold, to gather together the several threads that have brought the artists there, and to gaze with them (half-dumb, I am afraid) at the wondrous thing that still awaits accomplishment.

I

I think I see spread before me a new dramatic map of America. It is not like the old one—which appeared so strangely like an octopus, with its bulk over New York and its arms stretching out to Canada and Texas and the West coast. Instead there are many independent centers. Each represents, I am told, a native playhouse which is concerned with the art of the theater, just as in these same cities there are galleries concerned with painting and sculpture, and libraries concerned with serious literature. The buildings are individually beautiful, and one recognizes instinctively that they are *theaters*—that is, not amusement halls, but places for seeing beautiful things on a stage. Some of these buildings are owned by small groups of artists and workers, others by larger groups of art-lovers, still others by organized audiences, and finally, a few by municipalities. They all are administered, however, through enlightened groups of artists, and each has its artist-director who is in full charge of staging. Each has a reasonable appropriation each year, sometimes coming entirely from admission fees, and sometimes partly from endowments; but always the funds are handled in a businesslike way through a business manager. And finally, the native playwright gets his chance along with Shakespeare and Synge and Maeterlinck—and, be it noted, he is writing plays not unworthy of the honor.

If you ask the artists in one of these playhouses, they will tell you that it grew on foundations laid years ago by a group of visionaries who founded an amateurish little theater; they were laughed at by the know-it-alls of the business theater, secure in the knowledge of traditional ways of doing things; but they learned gradually to discard the weaknesses of the amateur while retaining his love of the work, and they chose certain good things and certain good people out of the commercial theater without taking over any of the tricks and vulgarities of the commercial institution. And finally they became professionals of a finer sort than any employed by the businessmen, and their playhouse became recognized as something as necessary to the community as the art gallery or the library or the schools.

That is the ideal in general; and that will be the method of its coming.

If you ask me why I am confident that it will come, when we have not now a single example of a permanent art theater company housed in a perfect home, with a reasonable appropriation and ideally organized, I can only point to the half dozen ventures I have mentioned so often, from Coast to Coast, and say that here are tangible evidences that many artists and some men of money have seen the new ideal. Indeed, that threshold is becoming a bit crowded. And just a few are crossing it, with timid feet, perhaps, and they are peering down one corridor after another. After a while, as more artists and more millionaires become interested, and when experience lightens the dark places a bit, they will step in boldly and become masters of the house.

A DISCURSIVE BIBLIOGRAPHY

A BIBLIOGRAPHY should be a guide from which the student can determine quickly where to turn for authoritative information about a given phase of a subject. But I have learned from experience that it usually is a list of titles of all books even remotely connected with that subject—a list that requires study in itself and leads into many false trails. The brief bibliography that follows makes no pretense to completeness. But I hope that it may serve, better than any hitherto published, to lead the reader to the *best* printed material (in English) about the progressive movement in the theater.

The pioneer among general works on the newer tendencies of theater art (as distinguished from drama alone) is Huntly Carter's *The New Spirit in Drama and Art* (New York: Kennerley, 1912). This contains first-hand accounts of theaters and methods of production in the principal European cities at a time when the ferment of new ideas was strongly at work. While the material is occasionally colored by Carter's individualistic theories, and is not closely coördinated, the chapters are invariably entertaining and remarkably suggestive. A more practical handbook of information about the progressive theater in its technical, artistic and literary aspects is Hiram Kelly Moderwell's *The Theater of Today* (New

York: Lane, 1914). This contains an immense amount of detailed material about modern plays, methods of staging, organization, etc. It remains, after more than a decade, one of the really indispensable volumes for students of and workers in the art theater. The third of the pioneer books which attempted to sum up modern tendencies was my own *The New Movement in the Theater* (New York: Kennerley, 1914). It may still afford the beginning student a useful perspective on the struggle for new types of play, for a new stagecraft and for a new theater architecture, but in general it seems to me outmoded.

Kenneth Macgowan's *The Theater of Tomorrow* (New York: Boni & Liveright, 1921) is by far the best existent summary of the progress of the art theater movement, with particular reference to methods of staging, and changing forms of stage and auditorium. It is profusely illustrated, and gives detailed information about technical devices as well as outlining modern theories of production and playwriting. It is the sanest and most useful treatise on the problems of the new theater, outside of acting. A journalistic summary of the progressive forces on the native stage is to be found in Oliver M. Sayler's *Our American Theater* (New York: Brentano's, 1923). A better-considered treatise on the beginnings of the struggle for a new theater in America is to be found in Thomas H. Dickinson's *The Insurgent Theater* (New York: Huebsch, 1917). This is a notably clear and reasonable record of the pioneer little and progressive theaters, with special reference to problems of organization.

Of books of theory, the most important is Gordon Craig's *On the Art of the Theater* (Chicago: Browne's Bookstore, 1911). The reader will find this remarkable volume pregnant with new ideas, and stimulating in its urge to get away from tradition and to do creative work in the theater. It is the most important source book of the new movement. *Towards a New Theater* (New York: Dutton, 1913) contains forty of Craig's designs, and its text is worth reading and then re-reading. The same is true of the book of reproductions of his etchings and its brief text: *Scene* (Oxford University Press, 1923). A number of Craig's short essays are collected in a volume entitled *The Theater—Advancing* (Boston: Little, Brown, 1919). This also will prove stimulating and provocative. There is no English translation of Adolphe Appia's important theoretical work *Die Musik und die Inscenierung*, nor is there even a fair extended transcription of his theories into English. A summary may be found in French in Jacques Rouché's *l'Art Théâtral Moderne*, (Paris: Cornély, 1910), which, by the way, is the most valuable French work on progressive theater methods. The new (1924) edition, it should be noted, is a cheap reprint, lacking the colored plates of the original. Since Appia is so important to students, and so neglected in English publications, I may add that two of his later essays are published in French: *l'Oeuvre d'Art Vivant* (Geneva and Paris:

Editions Atar, 1921), and *Art Vivant ou Nature Morte* (Milan: Bottega di Poesia, 1923).

There is much valuable material about theories of the theater scattered through Alexander Bakshy's two books: *The Path of the Modern Russian Stage* (London: Palmer & Hayward, 1916), and *The Theater Unbound* (London: Palmer, 1923). Bakshy often makes difficult reading—is not for the lazy-minded—but he is clearer than any other theorist in the matter of the presentational as against the representational theater. A useful compilation of dramatic theory and criticism before the modern era, from Aristotle to Brunetière and Archer, is *European Theories of the Drama*, by Barrett H. Clark (Cincinnati: Stewart & Kidd, 1918). The worker should read, too, H. Granville-Barker's *The Exemplary Theater* (Boston: Little, Brown, 1922).

Of the theories and achievements of Max Reinhardt there is a suggestive analytical account in Huntly Carter's *The Theater of Max Reinhardt* (New York: Kennerley, 1914). This treats incidentally of most of the theories and sources of the art theater movement, and is a book of prime importance. A later compilation of fugitive articles about Reinhardt and his work, ranging from the most valuable critical material to plain press-agent flattery, is to be found in *Max Reinhardt and his Theater*, edited by Oliver M. Sayler (New York: Brentano's, 1924). It is profusely illustrated.

Of special phases of modern theater development, the literary revival has received most attention from writers. Of interpretative accounts by far the best early work is Ludwig Lewisohn's *The Modern Drama* (New York: Huebsch, 1915), although one must make allowance for the author's bias toward Hauptmann and for an over-valuation of the realistic movement. A more scholarly and philosophical work, and one dealing extensively with the social implications of the new drama, is Archibald Henderson's *The Changing Drama* (New York: Holt, 1914). It is, however, not a good book for the beginning student. More in the nature of a textbook, or a simple reading guide, is Barrett H. Clark's *A Study of the Modern Drama* (New York: Appleton, 1925). It is international in scope, covering the work of sixty dramatists from Ibsen to O'Neill, and it contains useful and carefully prepared bibliographies. At the other extreme, but still concerned exclusively with the literary aspect of the theater, are these volumes of essays about individual dramatists: P. P. Howe's *Dramatic Portraits* (New York: Kennerley, 1913) and James Huneker's *Iconoclasts: A Book of Dramatists* (New York: Scribner's, 1905). More recent books about the drama and dramatists are Storm Jameson's *Modern Drama in Europe* (London: Collins, 1920), Ashley Dukes' *The Youngest Drama* (Chicago: Sergel, 1924), and Clayton Hamilton's *Conversations on Contemporary Dramatists* (New York: Macmillan, 1924). Isaac Goldberg has written an exhaustive and very useful book about the most modern tendencies in *The Drama of Transition* (Cincinnati: Stewart & Kidd, 1922). Thomas H. Dickinson's *The Contem-*

porary Drama of England (Boston: Little, Brown, 1917) is written from the progressive standpoint and is well worth reading.

Of material about individual theaters, too little has been put into book form. Ernest A. Boyd's *The Contemporary Drama of Ireland* is almost exclusively an account of the literary-amateur movement which resulted in the success of the Irish Players, and so makes stimulating reading for those interested in the non-commercial theater elsewhere. A more intimate and anecdotal account of the Abbey Theater group is to be found in Lady Gregory's *Our Irish Theater* (New York: Putnam's, 1913). Desmond MacCarthy's *The Court Theater, 1904–1907* (London: Bullen, 1907) is a suggestive account of the important Vedrenne-Barker art theater experiment in London. The *Deutsches Theater* finds extended treatment in Carter's *The Theater of Max Reinhardt*, mentioned above. Nothing could afford more interesting and stimulating reading for serious theater workers than Constantin Stanislavsky's autobiography, *My Life in Art* (Boston: Little, Brown, 1924), wherein the inspiring story of the Moscow Art Theater is told in detail. An outsider's view of the same theater, with important material about repertory, production and management, is to be found in Oliver Sayler's *The Russian Theater under the Revolution* (Boston: Little, Brown, 1920). The book also tells a great deal about the Kamerny and other important Russian theaters, and about the theories of Meyerhold and Yevreynoff. It is, indeed, one of the few very significant reportorial works on the modern movement. It is unfortunate that there are no translations of A. Thalasso's *Le Théâtre Libre*, which describes Antoine's experiment in detail, and Georg Fuchs' *Die Revolution des Theaters*, which is a statement of the principles upon which the Munich Art Theater was founded. A twenty-page excerpt from Antoine's Recollections was published in translation in *Theater Arts Monthly* for March, 1925, covering the exciting early days and the "first period" of the *Théâtre Libre*. A brief but valuable account of Copeau's founding and administration of the *Théâtre du Vieux Colombier* is to be found in Waldo Frank's *The Art of the Vieux Colombier* (Paris and New York: Nouvelle Revue Française, 1918). This essay is reprinted as a chapter in Frank's *Salvos* (New York: Boni & Liveright, 1924).

On the subject of modern stage decoration and production, the only general work of serious values is *Continental Stagecraft* (New York: Harcourt, Brace, 1922). It is a remarkably suggestive account of contemporary decorative practice in European theaters, as seen by Kenneth Macgowan and Robert Edmond Jones, with more than forty of Jones' drawings. In this connection students should study the two books of collected designs by Gordon Craig, already mentioned. They will be interested too in Norman-Bel Geddes' *A Project for a Theatrical Presentation of the Divine Comedy of Dante Alighieri* (New York: Theater Arts, 1924). The project is original and thought-provoking, and the book is finely illustrated. In a small corner of this special field, that of production out-of-doors, I wrote a book which at least has the virtue of profuse illustrations: *The Open-air Theater* (New York: Kennerley, 1918).

Interesting material about theater organization may be found in Archer and Barker's *Schemes and Estimates for a National Theater* (London: Duckworth, 1911). The repertory system is treated at some length in P. P. Howe's *The Repertory Theater, a Record and a Criticism* (New York: Kennerley, 1911). Percy MacKaye's two volumes, *The Playhouse and the Play* (New York: Macmillan, 1909) and *The Civic Theater* (New York: Kennerley, 1912), will prove suggestive rather than informative, but are worthy of attention. In order to know the organization of the business theater, and thus to learn many things to avoid and a few to copy, the progressive worker should read Arthur Edwin Krows' *Play Production in America* (New York: Holt, 1916). It is a remarkably complete and detailed account of the commercial theater as it exists, although it is colored by the author's desire to make out a case for the American producer as against the European.

There is no satisfactory book in English dealing with theater architecture. The so-called standard work, Edwin O. Sachs' *Modern Opera Houses and Theaters* (London: Batsford, 1908), is important historically, but is now entirely out-of-date in its treatment of both theater design and equipment. Material about the modern form of theater building is scattered, and is to be found only by laborious search through many German books and magazines. The matter is touched upon briefly in Moderwell's *The Theater of Today*, Carter's *The New Spirit in Drama and Art* and my *The New Movement in the Theater*. The technical aspects are treated at some length in Macgowan's *The Theater of Tomorrow*. A really admirable short essay on one phase of the subject is to be found in Irving Pichel's *On Building a Theater* (New York: Theater Arts, 1920). It treats primarily the problems of building little theaters and community house stages, but in the absence of other works written from the progressive viewpoint, it is invaluable to anyone studying theater design.

Current conditions in the American theater are best reflected, perhaps, in the collected dramatic reviews of Walter Prichard Eaton, Clayton Hamilton, Ludwig Lewisohn, George Jean Nathan and Stark Young. A more studied general review is to be found in certain chapters of Thomas H. Dickinson's valuable volumes *The Case of American Drama* (Boston: Houghton, Mifflin, 1915), and *Playwrights of the New American Theater* (New York: Macmillan, 1925).

Of periodicals the oldest and most provocative one dealing with the new theater exclusively is Gordon Craig's *The Mask* (Florence, Italy: The Arena Goldoni, 1908–1915, and 1923–date). This publication is full of that stimulating quality which marks all of Craig's writings, and it has already had great influence in shaping the progressive theater. *The Drama*, a *Quarterly Review of Dramatic Literature* (Chicago: The Drama League of America, 1911–1917) published much valuable material on the literary aspect, and occasional articles of a broader nature. Its successor, the present *Drama Monthly*, has been given up largely to material that interests the amateur little theater groups. The real mouthpiece of the workers in America's larger progressive theater —and with a worldwide circulation and influence—is *Theater Arts Monthly* (New York: 1916–date). In the revision of this book, I have found more pertinent material in the Theater Arts files than in all other publications together. I think that every student will find it extremely valuable as a reference work and as a source of inspiration and knowledge. No important progressive project fails to find description in its pages sooner or later, and its many illustrations are chosen with discrimination.

In writing my preface for this new edition, I became so interested in chronicling the changes in our American theater during the past decade, that I neglected to make the usual acknowledgments in that more proper position. I wish to correct the omission here. In the first place I must repeat my original acknowledgment of general indebtedness to Gordon Craig, Huntly Carter, H. K. Moderwell and the late William F. Gable. Beyond that I owe special thanks to several theater directors: Sam Hume, Maurice Browne, Irving Pichel, Frederic McConnell and Kenneth Macgowan. I wish to record particularly cordial thanks to Edith J. R. Isaacs, who not only helped me with material and suggestions, but read the entire book in manuscript.

INDEX

Abbey Theater, Dublin, 45, 58, 201, 272
Acting and actors, 44, 133
Acting, Effect of commercialization upon, 27
Actors' Equity Association, 76, 159
Actor's Theater, 7, 8, 17, 34, 57, 76, 84, 85, 103, 106, 128, 130, 148, 161, 179, 195, 208, 210, 221, 246, 250
Advertising, 247
Ames, Winthrop, 8, 9, 63, 99, 101, 142, 147, 161
Anglin, Margaret, 172
Antoine, André, 38, 39, 62, 273
Appia, Adolphe, 44, 55, 89, 120, 190, 269
Architecture, Theater, 30, 49, 253, 274
Art Theater: Definition, 11, 15
Artist-director, 43, 106, 236
Artists' Guild Theater, 234
Arts and Crafts Theater, 32, 65, 106, 122, 151, 163, 192, 204, 222, 234, 240, 244
Audiences, 17, 22, 208

Baker, George Pierce, 96, 131, 257
Bakshy, Alexander, 270
Barker, H. Granville, 40, 61, 197, 270
Barnes, Djuna, 68
Barrymore, John, 33
Beach, Lewis, 181
Beachwood Players, Scarborough, 182
Belasco, David, 6, 8, 161, 189
Benavente, 72
Bernhardt, Sarah, 137
Birmingham Repertory Theater, 60
Boleslavsky, Richard, 97
Boston Repertory Theater, 35
Boyd, Ernest, 272
Brady, William A., 18
Bragdon, Claude, 94, 188
Brahm, Otto, 38, 39
Brown, Gilmor, 126, 132, 155, 230
Browne, Maurice, 35, 37, 62, 94, 106, 118, 132, 142, 150, 151, 165, 259
Bryan-Allen, Martha, 147

Carb, David, 77
Carnegie Institute Theater, 96
Carolina Playmakers, 131, 182
Carroll, Albert, 148
Carter, Huntly, 50, 109, 140, 267, 270
Chicago Art Institute. *See* Goodman Memorial Theater
Chicago Little Theater, 32, 62, 65, 86, 106, 118, 151, 165, 172, 193, 199
Claire, Ina, 147
Clark, Barrett H., 270, 271
Classic plays, 169
Cleveland Playhouse, 32, 35, 62, 81, 97, 126, 155, 157, 167, 215, 257
Comédie Française, 16, 171, 184
Communi' theater: Definition, 213

Congreve, 7
Cook, George Cram, 68
Copeau, Jacques, 37, 54, 62, 106, 115, 117, 273
Cornell, Katharine, 147
Craig, Gordon, 37, 38, 40, 42, 51, 55, 58, 61, 63, 89, 94, 106, 119, 122, 190, 194, 200, 269, 275
Crothers, Rachel, 77, 169

Dakota Playmakers, 131
Dalcroze, Jaques, 120, 140
Dallas Little Theater, 35, 157
Daly, Augustin, 24
d'Annunzio, 174
Dell, Floyd, 68
Deutsches Theater, Berlin, 45, 52, 140, 272
deWeerth, Ernest, 188
Dickinson, Thomas H., 268, 271, 275
Digges, Dudley, 128, 148, 161
Drama League, 211, 225
Dramatists' Theater, 181
Duncan, Augustin, 37, 72, 126
Dunsany, 88, 138, 174

Eagels, Jeanne, 147
Eames, Clare, 128, 147
Eaton, Walter Prichard, 31, 77, 136, 275
Eldridge, Florence, 147
Endowment, 249
Entrikin, Knowles, 184
Equity Players: *See* Actors' Theater
Euripides, 88, 165, 170
Everyman Theater, 61
Experimental theaters, 95
Expressionism, 175

Fehling, Jurgen, 221
Fireside Players, White Plains, 215
Fiske, Harrison Grey, 9
Flavin, Martin, 184
Fontanne, Lynn, 147
Frank, Waldo, 56, 273
Freeman, Helen, 72, 147
Freie Bühne, Berlin, 39, 40
Frohmans, The, 9
Fuchs, Georg, 38, 51, 117, 273

Gahagan, Helen, 147
Gale, Mrs. Lyman, 64
Galesworthy, John, 8, 40
Garden Players, 157
Geddes, Norman-Bel, 33, 37, 94, 188, 236, 259, 273
Gillmore, Margalo, 147
Glaspell, Susan, 68, 184
Goethe, 117
Goldberg, Isaac, 271
Golden Bough, Theater of the, 35, 122, 256
Goodman, Edward, 130
Goodman Memorial Theater, Chicago, 35, 234, 256
Gorelik, Max, 188
Gorky, Maxim, 47
Greek Theater, Berkeley, 125, 170, 172
Greenwich Village Theater, 70
Gregory, Lady, 272
Grein, J. T., 39
Gribble, Harry Wagstaff, 167

Hamilton, Clayton, 271, 275
Hamlet, 51, 201
Hampden, Walter, 172
Hapgood, Norman, 31
Hasenclever, 175
Hauptmann, 174, 220
Hayes, Helen, 147
Head, Cloyd, 94, 184
Helburn, Theresa, 161, 230
Henderson, Archibald, 271
Herndon, Richard, 33
Hopkins, Arthur, 8, 9, 129, 142, 199

Horniman, Miss, 59, 250
Howard, Sidney, 7, 184
Hughes, Hatcher, 7, 69
Hull House Theater, 224
Hume, Sam, 37, 106, 122, 151, 163, 204, 222, 230, 234, 259

Ibsen, Henrik, 7, 39, 77, 78, 174
Independent Theater, London, 39
Indianapolis Little Theater, 32
Irish Players, 37, 55, 58, 128, 141, 143, 151, 155, 177, 178, 201, 250, 272
Irving, Henry, 228

Jackson, Barry V., 60
Jessner, Leopold, 62, 117
Jones, Frederick, 188
Jones, Robert Edmond, 33, 37, 69, 94, 129, 188, 195, 199, 273
Jonson, Raymond, 199
Jouvet, Louis, 60

Kahn, Otto, 74
Kaiser, Georg, 175
Kammerspiele, Berlin, 54
Kaufmann, Oskar, 260
Kayssler, Friedrich, 221
Kemp, Harry, 68
Kennedy, Charles Rann, 7, 78, 169, 226
Kenyon, Charles, 184
Koch, Frederick, 131, 157, 182, 224
Kreymborg, Alfred, 68
Krows, Arthur Edwin, 238, 274
Kummer, Clare, 168

Laboratory Theater, New York, 97
Lawrence, Margaret, 147
Lawson, John Howard, 7, 77, 176, 184
LeGallienne, Eva, 147
Lenihan, Winifred, 147
Lewisohn, Ludwig, 271
Lighting, 198, 258
Linnebach, Adolf, 62, 117
Little Theater, New York, 101, 255
Little theaters, 4, 31, 33, 130, 149, 200, 212, 237
Littmann, Max, 30, 257, 260
Lobero Theater: *See* Santa Barbara
Lord, Pauline, 147
Los Angeles Little Theater, 32, 192, 236
Loving, Pierre, 215

Macdermott, Norman, 61
Macgowan, Kenneth, 37, 69, 199, 230, 268, 273
Mackaye, Percy, 101, 184, 213, 274
Maeterlinck, Maurice, 47, 88, 138, 174, 196
Mapes, Victor, 119
Martyn, Edward, 58
Matthison, Edith Wynne, 137
McClintic, Guthrie, 142
McConnell, Frederic, 37, 81, 126, 150, 155, 230
Mielziner, Jo, 188
Millay, Edna St. Vincent, 68
Milne, A. A., 168
Milton, Robert, 130
Moderwell, Hiram K., 267
Moeller, Philip, 130
Moise, Nina, 126
Moliere, 170
Molnar, Franz, 7
Monck, Nugent, 60
Moody, William Vaughn, 226
Moore, George, 58
Morris, Mary, 147, 148
Moscow Art Theater, 11, 19, 40, 46, 96, 120, 140, 148, 155, 196, 201, 232, 242, 250, 272
Munich Art Theater, 45, 49, 273

Neighborhood Playhouse, 7, 8, 32, 35, 62, 65, 86, 148, 176, 224, 226, 250, 255
New Theater, New York, 63, 66, 250
Norwich Players, 60
Nyemirovitch-Dantchenko, 49

Oenslager, Donald, 188
O'Neil, Raymond, 37, 81, 126
O'Neill, Eugene, 7, 33, 35, 68, 69, 168, 181, 184
Organization, 228

Paris Opera House, 254, 256
Pasadena Community Playhouse, 35, 80, 126, 132, 155, 168, 215, 217, 255
Peters, Rollo, 37, 72, 188, 194
Pichel, Irving, 37, 126, 150, 259, 275
Pirandello, Luigi, 174
Platt, Livingston, 188
Players' Workshop, Chicago, 32
Playfair, Nigel, 60
Playhouse, Berkeley, 126
Playwriting, 26, 178
Poel, William, 60, 172
Portmanteau Theater, 32
Povah, Phyllis, 147
Prairie Playhouse, Galesburg, 32, 225
Provincetown Players, 7, 8, 27, 32, 35, 62, 66, 86, 96, 104, 106, 129, 148, 168, 181, 199, 210, 226, 250

Ram's Head Players, Washington, 35
Realistic drama, 41, 173
Reicher, Frank, 130
Reinhardt, Max, 45, 52, 57, 63, 92, 106, 109, 117, 270
Repertory, 10, 26, 184, 274
Reynolds, James, 188
Risdon, Elizabeth, 147
Robb, Lotus, 147
Robertson, Donald, 119
Roos, Joanna, 148
Rosse, Hermann, 188, 197
Rouché, Jacques, 45, 269

Santa Barbara Community Theater (Lobero Theater), 35, 80, 126, 234, 250, 256
Sayler, Oliver, 49, 242, 268, 270, 272
Schnitzler, Arthur, 174
Shakespeare, 47, 170, 173, 220
Shaw, Bernard, 7, 40, 62, 77, 157, 174
Shuberts, The, 18, 20, 157
Simonson, Lee, 33, 37, 73, 94, 188, 195, 197, 259
Stage Society, London, 61
Stagecraft, 28, 43, 186, 258
Stagers, The, 7
Stainslavsky, Constantin, 37, 46, 62, 106, 117, 272
Star System, 28, 144
Starke, Ottomar, 117
State Theater, Berlin, 62
Stevens, Thomas Wood, 35, 37, 131, 234
Stillman, Henry, 130
Stock Companies, 104
Strohbach, Hans, 221
Stylization, 93, 195
Subscription audiences, 217
Syndicate, 24
Synge, J. M., 55, 174, 177

Tchehoff, Anton, 47, 120, 226
Terry, Ellen, 63
Theater Guild, 7, 8, 17, 18, 34, 57, 71, 84, 96, 103, 106, 128, 148, 157, 161, 168, 181, 195, 208, 210, 221, 226, 246, 250, 255
Théâtre Antoine, 39
Théâtre de l'Oeuvre, 45
Théâtre des Arts, 45

Théâtre du Vieux Colombier, 45, 54, 62, 140, 273
Théâtre Libre, 38, 39, 273
Thomas, Augustus, 184
Thompson, Woodman, 188, 195
Throckmorton, Cleon, 188
Toller, Ernst, 175
Totheroh, Dan, 184
Toy Theater, Boston, 32, 64

Urban, Joseph, 188, 199

Volksbühne, Berlin, 18, 46, 62, 143, 175, 217
von Hofmannsthal, Hugo, 92, 112

Wagner, Richard, 117
Washington Square Players, 32, 68, 70, 86, 151, 181
Wenger, John, 188
Wilfred, Thomas, 94
Williams, Jesse Lynch, 77
Wilson, Edmund Jr., 69
Winwood, Estelle, 147
Wisconsin Players, 27, 32, 64, 96
Woods, A. H., 18, 157

Yeats, William Butler, 58, 94, 138, 143, 174, 177, 202
Young, Stark, 69, 275
Ypsilanti Players, 224
Yurka, Blanche, 147